living
WITHIN THE WILD

KIRSTEN DIXON
MANDY DIXON

ALASKA
NORTHWEST
BOOKS

Library of Congress Cataloging-in-Publication Data
is on file
ISBN: 9781513264370 (hardbound)
        9781513264387 (e-book)

Proudly distributed by Ingram Publisher Services

Printed in China
25 24 23 22 21 1 2 3 4 5

MIX
Paper from
responsible sources
FSC® C102842
FSC
www.fsc.org

Published by Alaska Northwest Books
an imprint of

WEST
MARGIN
PRESS

WestMarginPress.com

WEST MARGIN PRESS
Publishing Director: Jennifer Newens
Marketing Manager: Angela Zbornik
Project Specialist: Micaela Clark
Editor: Olivia Ngai
Design & Production: Rachel Lopez Metzger

Photo Credits: **MANDY DIXON:** Cover, Page 18, 35, 39, 45, 49, 61, 67, 68, 71, 72, 75, 76, 95, 96, 99, 104, 110, 114, 126, 129, 130, 133, 134, 150, 159, 160, 177, 178, 186, 199, 201, 202, 205, 208, 211, 214, 228, 232, 236, 239, 240, 243, 253, 259, 262, 269, 277, 281, 297 (top left); **SCOTT DICKERSON:** Page 1, 4-5, 6-7, 11 (middle right), 42, 46, 78-79, 121, 122, 166, 169, 195, 244-245, 260-261, 284-285, 297 (bottom), 304; **ASH ADAMS:** Page 2-3, 11 (middle), 12, 16, 21, 22, 28, 31, 32, 36, 50-51, 52, 55, 57, 58, 62-63, 83, 91, 100, 107, 108-109, 125, 142, 145, 146, 149, 153, 156, 163, 170, 173, 174, 181, 185, 189, 196, 202, 217, 218, 219, 220, 223, 227, 231, 235, 250, 296 (left and right), 297 (top right); **ALISSA CRANDALL:** Page 8; **CARL DIXON:** Page 11 (top row); **JEFF SCHULTZ/SCHULTZPHOTO.COM:** Page 164-65, 190-191; **TYRONE POTGIETER:** Page 11 (middle left), 19, 25, 26-27, 80, 87, 88, 138, 141, 192, 236, 270, 296 (top left); **NICK GRATTON:** Page 42, 103, 117, 182, 256; **KARYN MURPHY:** Page 110; **WES JOHNES:** Page 136–137; **STEPHANIE WELBOURNE-STEELE FOR *BAKE FROM SCRATCH*:** Page 224, 249

CONTENTS

I dedicate this book to my husband, Carl. We've been married to each other for more years than we have been apart. On the day you read your wedding vows to me, you said, "I will be your source of inspiration." And, you have been. And you still are. And, you will be as we grow old together.— **KIRSTEN**

I also dedicate this book to Carl, my father. You are not only the best father I could ask for, but you are one of the best humans I know. You have raised two girls to be thoughtful, kind, and respectful to the earth and to all living things and to be proud and confident women. You possess all the good qualities in a person and none of the bad. Thank you for being in all of our lives. All of us, every person you have taught to fly fish, to climb, to build, or to adventure, we are all better people because of you. Your moral compass points true north and that leads me forward. (P.S. Thanks for all the NTS.)— **MANDY**

A BLINK OF AN EYE

A NOTE FROM KIRSTEN

When we first married, Carl owned an Alaska river-rafting company. He would return from long trips to our home in Anchorage and tell me stories about his adventures—the blueberries along the banks of a particular river, the fishing, or what food he cooked over the campfire in the evenings. One night, while we were dreaming out loud to each other, we made the decision to seek a life lived close to nature. I wanted a garden with carrots that my babies could pull up from the ground, and Carl wanted to teach his children how to fish for salmon.

At that time, I was working in the ICU at the native hospital in Anchorage and Carl also had an audiology practice that required him to travel throughout Alaska. We wanted more time together. We wanted to live in the bright middle of life, where people were happy and eating together at the table, living robustly. The weight of working with critically ill or injured people, many facing the end of life, was too difficult for me to bear.

In the fall of 1983, we climbed into a float-equipped Cessna-206 airplane. I was two months pregnant. Along with our one-year old baby Carly, a black Labrador named Duncan, a broom and mop, and boxes of food, we headed out on our big adventure. The first snow had just begun to fall as we quietly glided onto the Yentna River, about 45 minutes north of Anchorage by air. We had found a piece of land to buy. We were going to make our living by starting a guest lodge.

That first winter, Carl and I led the simple uncomplicated lives we had been dreaming of. During the day, I kept the woodstove going and Carly fed while Carl worked on what would become the main building of the lodge we would open the next summer. In the evening, after the dishes were done, by the yellow glow of a kerosene lantern, we planned our new lives together.

In the depth of that winter, when the snow had fallen up to the windowsills, I would sink all the way up to my large and heavy belly if I walked off the trail. One day, there were people traveling along the river in a 100-mile cross-country ski race, then called the Iditaski. Racers stopped in to warm up and examine their gear. I baked them a blueberry pie.

> We wanted to live in the bright middle of life, where people were happy and eating together at the table, living robustly.

One racer happened to be a midwife and, as she ate her pie, she learned I hadn't had any medical care for my pregnancy. She had me lie down on the living room floor and she palpated the baby's position. She told me the baby was breech and she showed me special positions to sleep in to encourage the baby to turn.

In the springtime, in April, during the time of year when the river was jammed with ice that was too soft to land on, an old 1940s Piper PA-12 airplane landed on the tiny strip of sandbar in front of our cabin, with signs of spring already emerging everywhere out from the long winter. A friend hopped out and told me he was taking me to Anchorage right then and there. I was making him too nervous. Mandy was born two days later in the back bedroom of another friend's home. Our little family flew back to the river the next day. Carl had finished building our main log lodge he had worked on all winter and we moved out of our cabin and into our new home.

When Mandy was a newborn, I kept her in the crook of a Danish lounge chair just near the open-room kitchen where I worked. She was always swaddled up tightly and I would flip her over every so often. I would sit in the chair to feed and rock her. When Carly and Mandy were a little older, I'd put them both in highchairs and give them each a bowl of mashed potatoes to occupy themselves as I cooked. Mandy literally grew up in a kitchen.

> Eating well, enjoying life, meeting incredible people, being proud of our daughters, laughing all the time—these are our rich rewards.

The years went by and the girls grew older. They learned to fish. They could spin-cast and fly-cast. They held bloody beating salmon hearts in their hands. They drove boats as well as any fishing guide. They chopped kindling and kept a woodstove going.

We homeschooled Carly and Mandy over the long winters and they worked in the garden and in my kitchen through the summers. Mandy graduated from homeschool at seventeen years old, first in her class (and the only person in her class—it's a favorite family joke), and she immediately zoomed out of the state in a newly bought but slightly used Dodge Neon, down the Alaska Highway through Canada and off to California. Some years later, she returned home to her family business, to my deep relief. We've been cooking together ever since.

I've been collecting, curating, and writing recipes in some form or other my entire life. As a young girl I spent hours in the library reading through dusty volumes of people long gone, enjoying their stories of fêtes and feasts. Also, I always loved exotic cookbooks written by expats in faraway lands. I imagined the author and me dining together, talking about the day, the weather, or spices and herbs. I was hungry for communal nurturing and for a global understanding of others through their foodways. I carry that love and the love of culinary literature of all kinds to this day.

The past forty years together, first with Carl and then our small family, has gone by so quickly, seemingly in a blink of an eye. Carl and I are proud of how we have lived, how we have worked hard, and how we have served our guests and nurtured our family. Eating well, enjoying life, meeting incredible people, being proud of our daughters, laughing all the time—these are our rich rewards.

Writing about food isn't just scratching a recipe onto a grocery slip or transposed from the back of a can. It's documentation of our having been here, of having lived. It's the written witness of our times—for the hope of those meals we will prepare together in the future. Writing about food is an intimate conversation occurring between one cook and another through time and space. This collection of stories and recipes represents just a blink of time during our lives at Winterlake Lodge, Tutka Bay Lodge, and La Baleine Café, with the Dixon family.

AN IMMEASURABLE LIFE

A NOTE FROM MANDY

I grew up on a riverbank in a remote part of Alaska—no roads, no television, no Internet, no running water. But salmon and other fish filled our rivers, and our garden was full of giant vegetables from the midnight summer sun. Our water was clean and pure and cold, pumped straight from the ground. My playground was an endless forest of imagined castles and kingdoms.

My family lived above the main room of the little fishing lodge my parents built the year before I was born. Riversong Lodge is on the banks of the Yentna River, a glacial stream fed by beautiful winding rivers, big and small, known for abundant salmon. We hosted guests from around the world who would fish with my dad, and eat meals my mother would cook for them.

The summers for my sister and me were filled with fishing, driving boats up fast-moving rivers, navigating the woods with no trails, learning to forage edibles, and taking care of the garden. There were a handful of other families that lived along the river with kids the same age as us. We all knew how to drive a boat at seven years old and how to fix the boat's engine by our ninth birthdays. We loved to meet up on hot summer days and play on the glacial silt beaches of the river.

In the winters, we guided guests for skiing and snow machine rides, and we served as a checkpoint for a few human-powered races. But they were much quieter seasons. My family stayed warm in the log cabin, which was heated with a wood-fired stove. My dad taught me to cut down trees and how to make kindling to start fires properly. My mother taught me how to make bordelaise sauce.

My sister and I were homeschooled through the State of Alaska Correspondence school program. We were sent packets of schoolwork through the mail each month, and we'd drive a snow machine seventeen miles up the river to the post office to retrieve them. We had subjects in math and science, history, and literature. We learned social studies, music, and P.E. We both took French language and art as our electives. It was at our own pace, and there were no rigid school times or loud bells ringing to signal when it was time to play or eat. We did have a routine, and my parents were fairly strict with chores and staying on track with our schoolwork. And we did. I graduated from high school a year early and then went on to culinary school. But that's a story for another time.

> My playground was an endless forest of imagined castles and kingdoms.

Winters were quiet with just my family at the lodge. Shoveling the roofs of the cabins and keeping things from freezing were big chores. When spring came around, and the river ice began to break up, we would hire a small team of guides, housekeepers, dishwashers, and cooks to help us with the busy summer season.

When I was little, I used to be afraid of the chefs in the summer kitchen. They always seemed to be rushing around with hot pots of bubbling liquids or chopping something fiercely with a large sharp knife.

I walked around, shoeless most of the summer with dirt-stained, thick-skinned soles. Being barefoot, of course, was a problem for entering the sacred kitchen area where the cookie dough was kept. I became an expert at stealing cookie dough balls until one day I was caught by my mom, who was cooking in the kitchen. She grabbed my hand and said, "gotcha!" I was so scared that I was going to be grounded for the rest of the summer season. Then she released my hand and said with a calm voice and a smile, "Would you like to learn how to make them? You will have to put some shoes on and wash your hands first."

I was relieved and excited to be able to learn from the big, scary chefs. My mom helped me to be comfortable in the kitchen environment and how to work and learn with these chefs—chefs that stayed with us as guests, chefs that worked or interned in our kitchens, or chef-friends of my mother's who would come to visit and cook with us. Eventually, I was in charge of making cookie doughs and then desserts, and, finally, I was old enough to go to culinary school to gain even more of a culinary foundation for my life as a professional chef.

> I wish everyone could experience the immeasurable life I've been fortunate to live in Alaska.

I am thankful to have created this book with my mother. She is always the first to support me in anything I do and the first to inspire me to dream big and dare to fail. While working on the last cookbook together in 2013, we were devastated to learn Kirsten was diagnosed with triple-negative breast cancer, an aggressive cancer that required surgery and chemotherapy right away. My mother had a difficult summer, feeling ill and losing all her hair, but she stayed grounded in writing the book and testing recipes with me. Kirsten stayed in the "land of the living," as she would say. And, that she did. She had been cancer-free for six years when we found a new tumor, this time in her brain. It was in February of 2019, and we were well into writing and recipe testing for this book. Again, she would have to be strong, listen to the doctors, listen to her family, face death, and write a cookbook. And again, she did. We decided to undergo a treatment called CyberKnife to eliminate the cancerous tumor, and, lucky for us, there was a trained oncologist in Anchorage with the equipment and training. Again, we went through a difficult summer with an unknown future. Incredibly, and to our great joy, the CyberKnife treatment eradicated the tumor. We are thankful to be moving forward. I believe my parents' philosophy on life and how they have chosen to live their life in such a creative way has played a significant role in the recovery of my mother.

I appreciate my parents for allowing me to grow up in an amazingly rich environment, rich with great people teaching me lessons in life all along the way. Rich with a caring family that is proud, adventurous, and nurturing. Rich with adventure every single day.

I wish everyone could experience the immeasurable life I've been fortunate to live in Alaska. I hope everyone could step on a mountain where no human has stepped before, have an entire frozen, snowless lake for their private ice-skating rink, or ride behind a silent dog team gliding through the woods as it snows. The stories and recipes in this book will help you step into our world a bit. Perhaps one day you, too, will find your way to this magical part of the world.

OUR KITCHEN PHILOSOPHY

Our recipes are snapshots in time and place. They are the stories of the moment we share with you, but likely, even by the time you are reading this, we've evolved and changed in some subtle ways in what we are fascinated with, what we've learned through travel and experiences, and how we present our food. But a few things hold true in our kitchen:

TELL A STORY: The dishes we share mean something to us. They hold some memory, or flavor or feeling, or perhaps even a dream we've had that we want to convey to our guests. We are communicating the story of our experiences with others. We want others to "feel" our love of the place where we live through our food like they might through a poem or a story or a song.

HUMILITY SETS US FREE: We aren't above anyone in our understanding of food or cooking. We are in service to those we feed. Food can be used as a cultural symbol of who people are, what status they hold, and even what they believe in religiously. For our family, we've lived most of our lives far from these social dictates. We have been able to work hard against the backdrop of wildness not found elsewhere in the world. And, that has given us a rare kind of freedom.

ORGANIC, AS WE CAN: For a long time now, we make an effort to cook with natural, whole foods. It's easy to grow organically in Alaska. The soil in much of our inhabited state is fertile and free from pesticides and pests. As the world warms up, this might begin to change, but for now, we hardly amend our soil at all at the two lodges. The politics of food can be confusing, and choices about what to eat can be overwhelming. We have found the Environmental Working Group (EWG.com) to be a useful resource in deciphering some of the issues about what to buy absolutely organic and what may not be as necessary. We always buy, grow, or forage organic berries, cherries, strawberries, spinach, greens, and apples. We also use only organic tomatoes, potatoes, and celery. We aren't as fussed about buying organic cabbage, broccoli, or mushrooms. If you are looking for guidelines, find the annually updated list at EWG's website. And, we are reminded from time to time that just because something is labeled "organic" doesn't necessarily mean it is worth our trust, just as some things grown without an organic certification could be perfectly healthy and pesticide-free.

GROW OR HUNT OR GATHER AS WE CAN: Growing some part of our own food is essential to us, even if it is as small as a windowsill herb pot. We are lucky enough to have "high tunnels," greenhouses that we fill with herbs, tomatoes, and other culinary treasures that extend our growing seasons on both ends of our short, intense summers. We always have a few beds we dedicate to micro-greens for salads and garnishes. Most Alaskans seem to participate and take pride in some aspect of responsible food-gathering, whether it is dip-netting for salmon in the summer or taking a moose in the fall. We, as a family, and we, as Alaskans, have a strong undercurrent of self-reliance that is important in our food culture.

KEEP A CREATIVE PANTRY: Perhaps it reflects how we have lived for so long, but even in Anchorage, we both have significant pantry and food storage spaces. At Kirsten's house, it is an old walk-in closet near the back door that has been converted to hold shelves of dry goods, canned goods, and preserves (plus one shelf always filled with snacks for a young grandson). In the garage, we have metal racks that hold items bound for either one of the lodges or the café. At Mandy's condo, she has converted an empty bedroom into organized storage. We both adore any sort of pantry recipes like butters and chutneys, jams, jellies, and jars of this and bottles of that. We like a gleaming row of colorful glass jars filled with memories of our summers that we can open and share during our long winters.

NO SINGLE-USE PLASTICS: We began to get serious in the spring of 2019 to try to go plastic-free in all of our kitchens. That's not an easy ambition. We buy reusable, whimsical grocery bags from the Japanese grocery store in Seattle called Uwajimaya and a grocery store called Foodland in Honolulu. (Try to get your hands on some of these ever-changing and artistic collectible bags.) We love those deli-cups with good-fitting lids and plastic wrap for food storage, but we are saying goodbye to all single-use plastics in our lives. You'll notice lots of references to kitchen towels in this book vs. plastic wrap in our previous books. We no longer serve water in disposable plastic bottles or use plastic straws. These are small measures, we know, but they are important ones to move us forward to eliminating plastics in our lives.

SUPPORT OUR NEIGHBORS: There are many hard-working and remarkable, reliable farmers in Alaska, and we are particularly close to several family farms from the Mat-Su Valley near Anchorage and from the Homer area. We lean into our purveyors for their high-quality

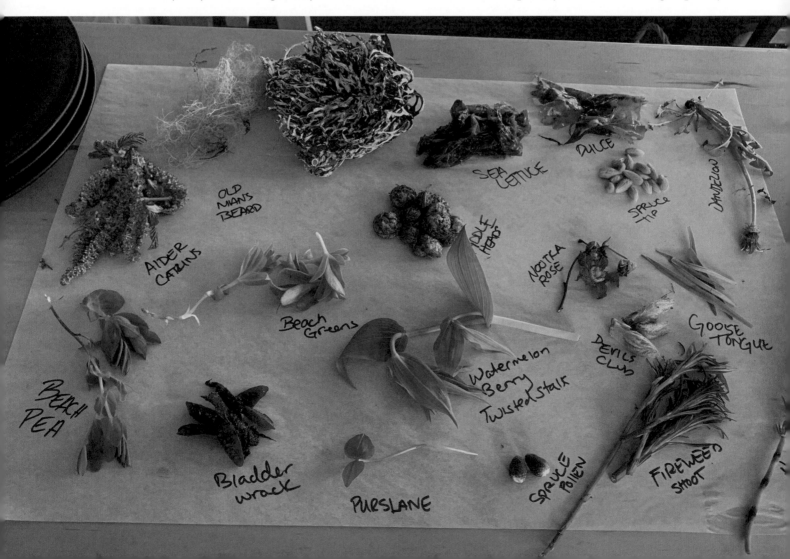

produce in the summer and storage crops in the winter. To support local growers and producers, we buy Alaska-grown foods over those from "outside" as much as we can, even if it means paying a premium price. With the advent of greenhouses, hearty farmers, a vibrant market culture, and Alaskans who care where their food comes from, the variety of available foods is expanding exponentially every year. We even have fruit growers who provide us with apples, cherries, berries, and more.

WASTE NOT: This is the same phrase as the title of a book published a few years ago by the James Beard Foundation featuring recipes that utilize foods that are typically thrown away. (We actually have a recipe in this collection.) We contributed the idea of scraping the meat from fish bones as we are filleting fish, commonly called "spoon meat." In general, we can collect as much as one pound of fish-meat from the carcass of an average-sized salmon, which we season up and make into a delicious burger or sauté and add to a pasta dish. This is such a small example, but we are committed to reducing our food waste.

BE GENEROUS: We prefer to live simply and without pretention, but we hope to feed our guests, our family, and staff with abundance and generosity. We don't save the best piece for last— we throw it into the mix and share with others. We don't care for cooks in our kitchen who feed themselves first or feed themselves better than others. "We can feed anyone at any time" is an ideal we aspire to.

KNOW WHO WE ARE: What kind of food do we make or aspire to create? Our food reflects our love of Alaska as a special wild place, our personalities, and our awareness of the future of food. When we travel, we often seek out Michelin-starred restaurants or award-winning kitchens of some acclaim, and we love studying fine-dining

cookbooks filled with lofty ideals and complicated dishes. We have both worked with, and learned from, world-famous chefs in intense kitchens, but we also aspire to cook at hawker stalls in Singapore and with old grannies in Italian basements making pasta. We want to experience it all and bring home the bits and pieces of creative learning that travel brings.

For the most part, modernist cuisine is the haute cuisine standard of our day, and we deeply admire this intellectual, precise style of cooking, but it is not entirely relevant to our rustic and wild kitchens. Just as a Wassily Kandinsky painting might look out of place on our log cabin walls, some styles of modern, urban plating might not fill the bellies of ravenous mountain climbers or ocean adventurers. Nor is modernist cuisine easy to execute in rural Alaska, given the sometime heavy-energy equipment use and labor intensity needed. BUT we enjoy taking elements of this and that—we have immersion circulators, hydrocolloids, and jars of alchemy to use in some of our dishes. We also have an old barrel woodstove that Carl made with stacks of alder wood next to it. As such, we move fluidly between ancient and modern culinary techniques, always staying on the terra firma of who we are.

So, what do we call our cooking? It's rustic, for sure. It's Alaskan, as we focus on Alaska ingredients. We are as passionate and intimate with our food (and, hopefully, as organized and clean in the kitchen) as any fine-dining chef might be. At the lodges, we prepare authentic cuisine bringing guests comfort at the table, where they can linger with each other in good conversation, and come to trust us. At the café, we bring big, hearty dishes to hungry fishermen and travelers, so that they can energize for their next adventure on the water. And, for our staff and families, we prepare meals that punctuate their long days of hard work with nourishing and exciting dishes they look forward to. So, what should we call our Within the Wild cuisine? Who knows—who cares—we simply want to cook.

A few more things you should know about this book:

- Even though we don't have the word *Alaska* plastered in front of each species of fish, we only use Alaska fish in our cuisine. The reason? We trust local fisher families and the cold, clear waters of Alaska.
- We prefer to use Alaska sea salt for most purposes, but we do buy kosher salt (Diamond Brand); fleur de sel from France as a finishing salt (Baleine brand—a nod to our love of France); sel gris (a wet mineral gray salt from France); and sometimes Maldon salt from the UK because we have a big chef-crush on Marcus Waring. (Kirsten also has a little crush on Harry Styles.) We also make our own sea salt from Tutka Bay (gather Alaska sea water, dehydrate—that's all there is to it).
- We still, after all these years, prefer to use unsalted butter in our cooking although we keep salted butter around as well. Salted butter is a preserved product (certainly handy at times), but unsalted butter is fresher with a cleaner flavor that we prefer.
- Mandy prefers vanilla paste in all her recipes, but Kirsten sneaked in "vanilla extract" in parentheses because she doesn't always "get" vanilla paste. It's a one-to-one conversion, so it's your choice. We always use pure vanilla.
- Most of our recipes using a vegetable oil state canola oil as our oil of choice, but you may wish to use any other type of neutral-flavored vegetable oil. We use grapeseed, olive oil, extra-virgin olive oils from Italy, Spain, France, Greece, and California, avocado oil, and lots of nut oils in our kitchens.
- In a couple of our recipes, you might notice we use granulated garlic instead of fresh garlic. This is purposeful for blending evenly. We make our own granulated garlic by dehydrating slices of garlic, then processing it in a food processor (see page 290). We also make garlic salt with our own sea salt and locally grown garlic. It's shelf stable and lasts a long time.
- We mention 4-quart and 6-quart casseroles quite a bit in our recipes—they are workhorses in our kitchens. These are similar to enamel-coated cast-iron pots (like Le Creuset or Lodge) and are heavy-duty to hold up to the heat of the propane burners we use. They are similar to Dutch ovens. You can certainly substitute whatever pot or pan works best for you.

LET'S JUST BEGIN OUR STORY HERE...

It's an early July morning in Southcentral Alaska. The sun is streaming through low-lying clouds as a gray fog shrouds the harbor. It's a moody weather day for summer, but perhaps it will improve later. La Balcinc Café, with its twinkling lights, is an inviting bright spot against the intense blues and grays of Kachemak Bay. If you peek inside one of the café windows, you'll see a warm and convivial scene of a room filled with fishers and locals, tourists, and weekenders from Anchorage. Mandy is cooking eggs and grilling salmon in the tiny kitchen.

The thing about owning a small café in a seaside town in Alaska is how quickly you learn to know the most colorful regulars. There's Breakfast Mike, who likes his egg sandwich cut in half so he can eat the other half later. And the Friday Morning Breakfast Club, a group of long-retired friends that meet once a week to talk about any adventures they've had. There's John, the owner of a bear-viewing guide boat who lives in Alaska year-round. He brings in his entire eclectic work crew for big meals. There's Don, who lives up on the mountain with his horses. He comes in almost every day for a plate of baked beans and greens. The cast of characters goes on, and they all breathe life into the place. The people who inhabit this space create a kind of kinetic energy that inspires Mandy to work hard, to do her best, and to be creative. She doesn't ever want to let these people down.

Across the bay, about twenty-five minutes by boat, Carly is setting out yoga mats onto the large wooden deck overlooking the ocean. The sun has broken through, and tiny beads of dew are evaporating around her. Grace Ridge, a 3,100-foot rise in the lush maritime landscape, looms just to the east of the lodge, displaying a hundred colors of green in the early morning light. The lodge is coming to life, hummingbirds dart in and out of the feeders surrounding the back deck, and the aroma of coffee fills the dining room. Carly faces her students and begins her morning routine, stretching and breathing in the salt-kissed morning air.

> **The sun is streaming through low-lying clouds as a gray fog shrouds the harbor.**

Down near the tide, naturalist guide and resident scientist, Karyn, is guiding a group of guests along the shoreline, pointing out creatures so small they would otherwise go unnoticed. Tiny oblong nudibranchs, mollusks that abandoned their shells a few million years ago, swirl amidst the bits of algae, amongst the anemone and sea stars. Karyn is gathering bright green sea lettuce into her basket to dry and use in the kitchen.

Later in the afternoon, another lodge naturalist guide will ready kayaks on the deck for the guests she'll take out after lunch. The group will silently paddle along the edge of the deep fjord of Tutka Bay into the Herring Islands looking for whales, sea otters, and the dozens of shorebirds pointed out along the way.

The thing about running a lodge in Alaska is that every little detail is essential. The lodge-based team is required to remember the arrivals and departures of the day, special requests, who is going bear-viewing or deep-sea fishing, which guests have special diets or want to go sea kayaking. They must organize and remember the menus of the day, which employees are off, what lodge chores need to happen. A thousand details are orchestrated, from music playing softly in the background to flowers on the table.

Kirsten is making her way along the tall wooden boardwalk that bridges the lodge and the cooking school, wrapping around the back lagoon. In her tote bag, she is carrying a new cookbook to add to the school collection, a few culinary items she's carried down from Anchorage, her black Moleskine notebook she carries everywhere, and packets to give to students for today's class. On the schedule: make a summer dish from the garden and a wild salad from foraged greens, topped with crab from the Bering Sea. But Kirsten is not quite as "in the moment" as Carly is. On her mind, as she walks along to the school, is the sizzling sake-yuzu dumplings she wants to make later in the day for appetizer hour.

> The thing about running a lodge in Alaska is that every little detail is essential.

At both Tutka Bay Lodge and to the north of Anchorage, at Winterlake Lodge, managers are overseeing final touches to the morning guest tables; herbs are picked from the garden to press gently into butter; fresh juice is squeezed; and napkins are folded just so. These and other small luxuries of lodge life are practiced throughout the day, the small grace notes to the rhythm of our lives.

Kirsten and Mandy will fly later in the week to Winterlake, where the lodge flora and fauna (and the menus) are entirely different than its seaside sister. In summer, the landscape at Winterlake is splashed with rich, vibrant greens and thick ribbons of steel-blue riverbeds that braid across the valley. And, in the winter, deep white snow glitters against pink and blue skies, showing off a low-lying winter sun. Winterlake is surrounded by spruce and birch forests and a million-acre mountain range that feels like a private park. All things here are about the dense forests, the sled dogs, the bears, and the sheer wildness of the land.

So, how do we, this adventurous and hard-working band of women, along with our equally formidable male counterparts, a precocious, third-generation Alaskan boy, as well as twenty sled dogs, manage to run two far-flung lodges, one busy café, and a cooking school? It's a piece of cake. Literally. Our favorite cakes that get us through any situation:

Zucchini Cake with Miso Glaze (page 118)
Lemon Honey Cake with Ricotta (page 158)
White Russian Coffee Cake (page 225)
Steamed Chocolate Beet Cake (page 233)
Black Currant Jam Cake (page 238)

Our solution for stress or worries: pick any one of the above cakes, find the recipe in this book, gather, scoop, stir, pour, and bake. Then, sit down at a table with a lovely view, and glide a fork through a healthy slice. Take in a deep breath and realize that nothing is quite as busy or bad as it may seem.

Join us through these stories as we share our lives with you, as we describe why we have chosen to live in this often harsh and still-wild place, close to nature, away from many of the luxuries of the modern world.

SPRINGTIME IN THE HARBOR

When we first bought a building on the Homer Spit, that lively piece of land that juts out over Kachemak Bay, it was in the depth of winter. The shuttered buildings lined either side of the Spit, and the beach was empty and moody, with large waves crashing against sand and rocks. Everything was washed in deep blues and greys in every possible degree of intensity.

We brought down a couple of Japanese-style butane burners to cook on, and sleeping bags and pillows. Carl and Neil did the heavy work of lifting, repairing, and painting, and we all slept on the floor of what would eventually become a little lifestyle store called Rustic Wild.

For the first meal we prepared, we set up our burners on a worktable outside. Immediately, eagles swooped around us, grabbing bits of burger and buns. We gasped and screamed, then laughed and scrambled for our cameras. It was an introduction to our new life in the harbor.

The winter gave way to spring, with a million birds appearing and gulls lining the balcony of our little building. Vans and minivans and trucks showed up filled with T-shirts and mugs and other such stuff for all the small colorful stores coming to life. The haunting gray sea gave way to a bright liquid playground where kitesurfers and boats and stand-up paddleboards twinkled and moved in the reflection and motion of the water. Our store was adorable, and we loved it.

After a year or so, we purchased the small building in front of the Rustic Wild. We named it La Baleine Café, a nod to our French culinary training—and to all the whales in Kachemak Bay. We needed prep space for our more labor-intensive style of cooking, and so that was the prompt end of our retail adventure. Mandy moved in a big hardwood worktable that had been in our kitchen at Riversong Lodge back in the eighties, and we packed away our lotions and linens and scarves. We found some shelving and

fridges, and suddenly a team of young people was chopping and dicing and playing reggae music, sending out trays and tubs of this and that to keep the café stocked.

On our first day of business at La Baleine, we weren't quite sure if anyone would even come through the front door. One person stopped in, and then another. We figured out how to play music over our iPod, how to use the checkout system. We ran around the Spit picking wildflowers for the tables and bought a few pieces of art to go on the walls. The whole thing was an adventure. If you go into the café now, you see six or seven employees, with more in the back prepping. On that first day, there was a sum total of two.

The harbor seems to be in perpetual motion.

Over time, we bought another building and then another. Eventually, we had a small enclave surrounding the café with housing for a few workers, storage for our dry goods, and a scruffy courtyard of grass and picnic tables where the crew could take a break. We met our neighbors, L.B., a bartender at the Salty Dawg; Billy, the fishmonger behind us; and Mako, the water taxi guy. And, over the years, these people have become friends and a kind of family, as have many of the patrons of our little café.

Behind us, the harbor lights always seem to be on. Vessels of every size and shape, from massive ocean-crossing ships to small skiffs, line the harbor's boat slips and transient rails. The harbor seems to be in perpetual motion. Boats are on the move, and people are traveling up and down the steel ramps that lengthen—sometimes with alarming steepness—and shorten with the tides.

In May, the Spit comes alive with people in shorts and sunglasses, with maps and cameras, walking up and down through the shops finding local treasures like whale-bone earrings or handmade pottery. There's a shop that cooks artisan pizza in a wood-fired oven and one that makes gelato like it is straight from Italy. There's also plenty of deep-fried fish and chips, fresh oysters, and crabs sold by the pound.

The constant noise of the harbor is comforting in some strange way, a reassurance that the ocean is still healthy with plenty of fish out there to catch. From our apartment window, we can see fishers off-loading their freshly-caught precious freight late into the night, craned up from boat holds into huge crates of chipped ice, then loaded onto trucks and whisked off bound for who-knows-where, maybe Seattle or Tokyo. During the early hours, supplies are loaded down to boats in big nets, provisions of all kinds to outfit some exciting new trip. Going out to sea to catch fish to feed the world is hard physical and never-ending work, and we are appreciative of bearing witness to it all.

> The constant noise of the harbor is comforting in some strange way, a reassurance that the ocean is still healthy with plenty of fish out there to catch.

Next door to the café, Billy Sullivan expertly fillets fish all day long and packs them into ice and boxes, then loads his wares onto a bicycle delivery vehicle and travels along the Spit, making fresh-from-the-boat deliveries. We buy fresh rockfish and halibut from him all summer. Sometimes Billy gives us bags of halibut "spoon meat," which we use in burgers served with cherry chutney. Local farmer Lori stops in and gives Mandy her weekly order of greens and garlic, tomatoes, and pea shoots, and whatever other offerings she has. Mandy takes what Lori brings and weaves the produce into her menus. Out of the back door, there are buckets of food scraps from Tutka Bay Lodge as well as the café waiting for a local farmer friend to pick them up for compost and feeding his livestock.

Today, it is 5:30 in the morning at the start of our spring season. The sun is following its northeast high-latitude circuit and is just rising. Fishermen are already preparing to go out onto the ocean for the day. At La Baleine, coffee is ground, thick gravy is made to pour over fat, fluffy biscuits, and the black beans are scented with cumin, ready for musher's meals and burritos. The flat-top griddle is flipped on and garlic butter is melted to brush onto the telera rolls we use with egg sandwiches. The display case is filled with muffins and breakfast bread. The café will hum throughout the day with salmon bowls and ramen bowls, fish and local vegetables piled high onto breakfast and lunch dishes, all passed through the tiny opening of the kitchen to the dining room. Mandy reaches over the sandwich prep counter and turns on the neon Open sign. As she heads to the front door to unlock it, a fisherman reaches for the outside handle and gives it a twist. So begins our season in the harbor on the Homer Spit.

WILDFLOWER SEMOLINA PANCAKES

We make two kinds of semolina pancakes: big fluffy ones like these, and thin, flat, yeasted ones like cooks make in Morocco. Both are equally delicious with our Alaska honey. We like to put delicate, edible wildflowers into these pancakes for a special, colorful, springtime touch and serve them with plenty of butter and perhaps a drizzle of Alaska birch syrup or honey.

MAKES 10 PANCAKES

1 cup all-purpose flour	2 large eggs
1 cup fine semolina flour	3 tablespoons butter, melted and cooled
2 teaspoons baking powder	Juice of ½ orange
½ teaspoon sea salt	Finely grated zest of 1 orange
½ teaspoon baking soda	Canola oil for the griddle
1½ cups buttermilk	½ cup edible wildflowers, stems removed
1 tablespoon honey	

Preheat the oven to 225°F. Line a baking sheet with parchment paper.

In a bowl, whisk together the flour, semolina, baking powder, salt, and baking soda. In a separate bowl, combine the buttermilk, honey, eggs, melted butter, and orange juice. Pour the buttermilk mixture into the flour mixture and mix only until just combined. Gently stir in the orange zest.

Heat a 12-inch nonstick griddle over medium heat until a drop of water sizzles on the surface. Brush the griddle lightly with some oil. Scoop ¼ cup of the batter onto the griddle, spreading it out to 4 inches. Repeat to add additional pancakes to the griddle surface. Lightly sprinkle some of the wildflowers over each pancake as you begin to cook. Cook until the pancake surface is bubbly, and the edges are dry, 2 to 3 minutes. Using a spatula, flip the pancakes over and cook until golden on the bottom side, about 2 minutes. Transfer the pancakes to the prepared baking sheet. Keep the pancakes warm in the oven until ready to serve.

Repeat cooking using the remaining batter and wildflowers. Serve right away.

SALMON SCOTCH EGGS

Kirsten won a trip to Osaka, Japan, years ago by submitting this recipe. She went back several times with the same hosts, Hankyu Corporation. She prepared Alaska seafood dishes during cooking demonstrations in a beautiful grocery store called Hankyu Oasis. This recipe is still a bar appetizer favorite at the lodges, or we sometimes slip these into packed to-go lunches for skiers.

MAKES 4 SERVINGS

5 extra-large eggs, at room temperature

1 lemon

½ pound skinless sockeye salmon fillet

½ pound hot-smoked (kippered) salmon

1 tablespoon Dijon mustard

1 tablespoon mayonnaise

1 teaspoon hot pepper sauce

Sea salt and freshly ground black pepper

¼ cup minced fresh flat-leaf parsley

1 tablespoon finely diced red onion

½ cup all-purpose flour

½ cup panko breadcrumbs

Canola oil for frying

Soy sauce for serving

Bring about 1 inch of water to a boil over high heat in a pot with a lid. Reduce the heat to medium-high, add 4 of the eggs, and cover with the lid. Boil the eggs for 7 minutes. Meanwhile, prepare a bowl of ice water. Use a slotted spoon to transfer the eggs to the ice water to stop them from cooking. Peel the eggs and pat them completely dry.

Finely grate the zest from one-half of the lemon. Cut the other half into wedges and set aside. In a food processor, combine the fresh salmon, smoked salmon, lemon zest, mustard, mayonnaise, and pepper sauce until a rough, not-too-fine paste forms. Transfer the salmon paste to a bowl. Mix in the parsley and onion and season to taste with salt and pepper.

Divide the salmon mixture into 4 equal portions. Flatten one portion in the palm of your hand and gently fold and push it around

1 cooked, peeled egg until completely covered. Repeat with the remaining eggs and salmon mixture. Set aside.

Put the flour into a wide, shallow bowl and stir in 1 teaspoon each of salt and pepper. Crack the remaining egg into another shallow bowl and whisk. Put the breadcrumbs into a third shallow bowl. One by one, dip the salmon-coated eggs into the flour, then the egg, and finally the breadcrumbs. Place the prepared eggs on a plate.

Fill a 4-quart pot with 1½ quarts of oil and heat over medium-high until it reads 350°F on a deep-frying thermometer. Fry the Scotch eggs in the hot oil until deep golden brown, about 5 minutes. Drain on paper towels. Serve with the lemon wedges and soy sauce.

SEAWEED YEAST POPCORN SEASONING

Friday nights are popcorn night. At the lodges, we share a good movie with our crew, and at the café we have live music. Everyone loves our seaweed popcorn, especially with a splash of melted butter. The combination of seaweed and nutritional yeast are an umami bomb that is delicious on almost everything from crackers to ice cream. Kirsten even likes this on hot buttered white rice with a splash of soy sauce for a simple and quick dinner. Look for seaweed flakes in a natural food store or from an online source.

MAKES 3 CUPS

1 cup seaweed flakes

1 cup nutritional yeast

½ cup ground dried mushrooms

½ cup granulated garlic

¼ cup sea salt

In a bowl, mix together the seaweed flakes, nutritional yeast, mushrooms, garlic, and salt. Keep in an airtight container for up to 6 months.

SALMON BOWL WITH MISO DRESSING

Salmon and miso are flavors that go together in our minds. This is a café recipe, but we often make it for lodge guests and staff. We use vegetables from both our garden and the local farmers market, so the choices are ever-changing through the summer. Try, as we do, roasted beets, turnips, and whatever vegetables you have on hand in place of the summer squash during the winter months. Make sure the salmon is brought to room temperature and patted dry before cooking.

MAKES 4 SERVINGS

FOR THE RICE

2 cups short-grain brown rice

3 cups water

1 teaspoon sea salt

FOR THE MISO DRESSING

¾ cup canola oil

1 cup plain yogurt

½ cup rice vinegar

¼ cup toasted sesame oil

2 tablespoons soy sauce

1-inch knob ginger, peeled and grated

4 cloves garlic, grated

1 tablespoon white or yellow miso paste

1 tablespoon sesame seeds, toasted

FOR THE ROASTED VEGETABLES

1 cup diced yellow squash

1 cup diced zucchini

1 small red onion, cut into ½-inch slices

1 cup quartered mixed mushrooms

4 tablespoons canola oil

Sea salt and freshly ground black pepper

¼ cup canola oil, plus more for cooking

4 (4- to 6-ounce) salmon fillets, skinned

2 cups mixed salad greens

¼ cup rice vinegar

¼ cup finely chopped mixed fresh herbs such as parsley, chives, and basil

To make the rice, place the rice, water, and salt into a wide 3-quart saucepan with a tight-fitting lid. Bring the mixture to a boil, cover, and reduce the heat. Cook until al dente, about 30 minutes. Let the rice stand for 10 minutes, covered, off the heat to absorb the steam. Fluff the rice with a fork.

To make the dressing, in a bowl, combine the canola oil, yogurt, vinegar, sesame oil, soy sauce, ginger, garlic, miso, and sesame seeds and whisk until emulsified.

To make the vegetables, preheat the oven to 425°F. Spread the squash, zucchini, onion, and mushrooms onto a parchment-lined baking sheet and drizzle with oil.Season lightly with salt and pepper. Toss to coat in the oil and seasonings. Roast the vegetables until lightly browned, about 15 minutes.

Place a large sauté pan over medium heat. Add 2 teaspoons canola oil to the pan. When the oil is hot, add the salmon fillets, skinned-side up. Cook for 3 to 4 minutes. Turn the fillets over with a metal spatula. Cook until the flesh is firm to touch, 3 to 4 more minutes. Brush 1 teaspoon of the miso dressing over the salmon. Set aside to keep warm.

To assemble, toss the greens with the vinegar and oil to taste. Season with salt and pepper to taste. For each bowl, place 1 cup of the cooked rice into a wide-rimmed deep bowl. Drizzle 2 to 3 teaspoons of the miso dressing over the rice. Top with some of the roasted vegetables. Add the dressed greens and sprinkle with herbs. Place a salmon fillet on top. Serve right away.

RHUBARB SALMON BACON

We make several different "salmon bacon" recipes, but this always comes in as a favorite. We serve it as an alternate to pork-based bacon. Recently, we had a departing lodge guest request a bag of this salmon bacon to travel home with. He lived in Africa!

MAKES ABOUT 10 SLICES

Canola oil for greasing

6 ounces cold-smoked salmon (lox), about 10 slices

½ pound rhubarb, washed, trimmed, and chopped

½ cup honey

½ cup apple cider, plus more if needed

½ shallot, sliced

Freshly ground black pepper

Preheat the oven to 350°F. Line a baking sheet with parchment paper or select a nonstick baking sheet.

Lay the pieces of salmon onto the baking sheet in a single layer. Set aside.

Place the rhubarb, honey, apple cider, and shallot in a small, heavy-bottomed saucepan. Heat over medium-low heat until the rhubarb is cooked and begins to fall apart, about 30 minutes. Add a little more apple cider if more liquid is necessary. The mixture should be reduced to a thick, syrupy consistency.

Brush the tops of the salmon slices with the rhubarb mixture. Sprinkle with black pepper to taste. Place the baking sheet onto the center rack of the oven and bake until the bacon is just crisp, 5 to 6 minutes.

Let cool completely before serving. Store in an airtight container between layers of parchment paper for up to 1 week.

BUTTERMILK BARLEY CORNBREAD

Barley couscous is a product easily found in Alaska, as it is made by an Alaska flour company. It comforts us that we have our own homegrown grain, as corn doesn't seem to proliferate at our latitudes. Nevertheless, cornmeal is always in our pantry and we use it in many dishes. We serve this cornbread with soups, hearty stews, and our Reindeer Chili (page 44).

MAKES 8 SERVINGS

Canola oil

1 cup yellow cornmeal

1 cup all-purpose flour

½ cup barley couscous, cooked according to package directions

1 teaspoon baking soda

½ teaspoon sea salt

1 large egg

1 cup buttermilk

2 tablespoons honey, plus more for brushing

⅓ cup peeled and finely diced yellow onion

½ cup flaked hot-smoked (kippered) salmon

¼ cup shredded white cheddar cheese

2 tablespoons sliced green onions

Unsalted butter for brushing

Preheat the oven to 350°F.

Grease a 10-inch cast iron skillet lightly with canola oil. Place the skillet on the stove top over low heat.

In a bowl, mix together the cornmeal, flour, barley couscous, baking soda, and salt. Add the egg, buttermilk, 2 tablespoons canola oil, honey, and onion. Mix just until the dry ingredients are moistened. Fold in the salmon, cheese, and green onions. Pour the batter into the hot skillet.

Place the pan onto the center rack of the oven. Bake until the top of the bread is well browned and the center is firm, 30 to 35 minutes. Brush the top of the cornbread with a little extra honey and butter.

Let cool slightly, then cut into wedges and serve.

CHERMOULA CRAB SALAD

This is a recipe given to us by Hicham Hnini, our chef-friend and Moroccan adopted family member. We like chermoula sauce on salmon, halibut, or vegetable salads. Serve this spiced salad on toasted bread, crackers, or a bed of crisp lettuce.

MAKES 4 SERVINGS

1 pound crabmeat, picked over for shells

3 cups fresh cilantro, roughly chopped

1 cup fresh flat leaf parsley, roughly chopped

8 cloves garlic, roughly chopped

1 teaspoon sea salt

½ cup fresh lemon juice

¼ cup extra-virgin olive oil

2 tablespoons water

1 tablespoon ground cumin

1 tablespoon sweet paprika

1 teaspoon harissa paste

1 teaspoon ground ginger

1 teaspoon ground turmeric

½ teaspoon freshly ground black pepper

Squeeze out any excess water from the crabmeat and put it in a bowl. Cover the bowl with Bee's Wrap and set aside at room temperature.

In a food processor, combine the cilantro, parsley, garlic, and salt. Pulse on medium speed to roughly blend the herbs and garlic. Add the lemon juice, olive oil, water, cumin, paprika, harissa, ginger, turmeric, and black pepper, and process until a rough paste forms. Pour the herb paste over the crab and gently toss with tongs to coat all of the crabmeat. Put the crab salad in the refrigerator for about 20 minutes.

Serve chilled.

BLACK BEAN REINDEER CHILI

We like to eat this over hot, freshly made Buttermilk Barley Cornbread (page 41) or steaming brown rice. Mandy even has a favorite ceramic bowl she prefers her black bean chili to be served from—it's just the right size to wrap hands around.

MAKES 6 SERVINGS

1 tablespoon canola oil

1 pound reindeer (or other) sausage, cut into ½-inch pieces

2 stalks celery, diced

1 carrot, peeled and diced

½ yellow onion, diced

4 cloves garlic, minced

1½ tablespoons honey

1 tablespoon instant espresso powder

1 tablespoon unsweetened cocoa powder

1 tablespoon pure chile powder

2 teaspoons ground cumin

2 teaspoons sea salt

½ teaspoon freshly ground black pepper

¼ cup fresh orange juice

4 cups homemade or store-bought chicken stock

2 cups crushed tomatoes

1 dried bay leaf

3 cups cooked black beans, drained and rinsed

Sour cream and sliced green onions for serving

Heat the oil in a 6-quart casserole over high heat. Add the reindeer sausage, celery, carrot, onion, and garlic. Turn the heat to low. Cover the pot and cook until the meat is browned, stirring occasionally, about 5 minutes.

Uncover the pot and add the honey, espresso powder, cocoa powder, chile powder, cumin, salt, pepper, and orange juice. Stir the spices into the vegetables, lightly toasting them in the oil. Add the stock, crushed tomatoes (with juices), and bay leaf. Cover the pot and simmer until the carrots are tender, about 7 minutes. Stir in the beans during the last 3 minutes of cooking time.

Divide the stew among serving bowls and serve hot with a dollop of sour cream and a sprinkle of green onions.

ALMOND RASPBERRY COFFEE CAKE

Raspberries are a summer indulgence. Since we grow them in our gardens, we use them with abandon in season. They grow so well here in the far north. In the winter, we can only dream about them. This cake is an early morning favorite. The banana and yogurt make the cake moist and extra flavorful. The almonds add a roasted note that goes well with a first cup of coffee.

MAKES ONE 10-INCH BUNDT CAKE; 12 TO 16 SERVINGS

⅔ cup unsalted butter,
    at room temperature

1½ cups sugar

3 large eggs

1 teaspoon pure vanilla bean paste
    or vanilla extract

3 ripe bananas, mashed

1 cup plain yogurt

1 teaspoon baking soda

2½ cups all-purpose flour

1 teaspoon baking powder

1 cup almonds, toasted and chopped

½ cup fresh raspberries

Preheat the oven to 350°F. Grease and flour a 10-cup nonstick Bundt pan.

In the bowl of a standing mixer fitted with the paddle attachment, cream together the butter and sugar, on medium speed, for about 30 seconds. Add the eggs and vanilla. Beat until fluffy. Add the bananas and mix well.

In a separate bowl, mix together the yogurt and baking soda. Let the mixture stand for 1 minute to activate the soda.

With the mixer on low speed, slowly add the flour and baking powder to the butter-banana mixture just until mixed. Remove the mixer bowl from the stand and gently fold in the yogurt mixture, ½ cup of the almonds, and the raspberries with a spatula. Sprinkle the remaining ½ cup almonds into the prepared Bundt pan. Pour the batter over the almonds into the pan. Bake until the cake is golden brown, appears to be set on top, and springs back slightly in the center when you press it, about 50 minutes. Let cool completely on a wire rack.

To unmold the cake, gently separate the cake from the sides of the pan using a paring knife if necessary. Place a large flat plate over the cake and carefully invert the pan to release the cake. Lift the pan away from the cake slowly, releasing any stuck bits if needed. Cut into slices and serve.

SESAME CHEESECAKE BARS

These are a perfect pick-me-up alongside a late afternoon coffee on the deck, watching the whales go by. Make sure you clear out a space in your freezer before you start. Serve these with Espresso Whipped Cream (page 289) and Sweet Sesame Crunch (page 293), or with fresh berries if you have them.

MAKES 24 BARS

FOR THE CRUST
2 cups almond meal
2 cups oat flour
¼ cup toasted sesame seeds
Pinch of sea salt
½ cup unsalted butter, melted
1 tablespoon honey

FOR THE FILLING
2¼ cups cream cheese,
    at room temperature
1 cup mascarpone cheese
¾ cup ricotta cheese
½ cup tahini
7 gelatin sheets, or
    7 teaspoons powdered gelatin

2 cups heavy cream
1½ cups sugar
Juice of 1 lemon
1 teaspoon pure vanilla bean paste
    or vanilla extract

To make the crust, line a 12-by-17-inch rimmed baking sheet with parchment paper. In a bowl, combine the almond meal, oat flour, sesame seeds, salt, butter, and honey. Mix well, then transfer to the prepared baking sheet, spreading it out evenly to the edges of the pan.

To make the filling, put the cream cheese, mascarpone, ricotta, and tahini into a food processor and pulse until smooth. Scrape the cheese-tahini mixture into a bowl. If using gelatin sheets, put them in a small bowl of iced water.

In a saucepan over medium heat, combine the heavy cream with the sugar and bring to a simmer. If you are using gelatin sheets, squeeze all the water from the gelatin sheets and add

them to the heavy cream. If you are using powdered gelatin, add it to the cream mixture. Turn off the heat. Stir the mixture several times to dissolve the gelatin. Strain the cream mixture through a fine sieve into a bowl. Slowly pour the hot cream mixture over the cheese mixture, whisking to incorporate. Mix in the lemon juice and the vanilla.

Pour the filling into the pan over the crust. Place the baking sheet into the freezer and let set for 30 minutes.

Using a large, sharp knife, cut the cheesecake into 2-by-4-inch bars. Bring the bars to room temperature before serving.

GIRLS' FISH CAMP

Our boat, the *Sea Salt*, crosses the entrance to Tutka Bay from Eldred Passage and pulls up to the edge of the dock. Kirsten has on her rubber boots decorated with colorful sea creature patterns, and Mandy is wearing her bright orange waterproof bibs. We've been fishing, and we talk excitedly as commercial fishers off-load bright, silvery salmon onto the shore. This moment, in some variation, has been happening in this exact spot for as long as humans have lived here.

Imagine life in Alaska a thousand years ago. Tutka Bay Lodge evaporates, and the uninterrupted landscape surrounding the bay is a deep lush green. Not much is different from the modern-day Tutka Bay cove except the tall, old-growth spruce forest that shades the sloping rock down to the ocean is much thicker and denser. Imagine that near the edge of the high tide rim, there is a small group of women working at a hearth built from mud and rock into the hill. The women are talking away, cleaning fish with stone tools, picking through berries, and separating herbs gathered in spruce root and seagrass baskets. The women are clothed in waterproof skins to protect themselves from the maritime weather, birch-bark bowls sit near the hearth, and children are playing in the semi-subterranean dwelling nearby, nearly undetectable against the forest floor. The prehistoric life is balanced, ordered, and peaceful. There are stories to tell in the evening about how the Earth was formed and how there is a responsibility to care for fish in the ocean. It's a long time before any Russians arrive.

And, here we are in the present, standing in the same Tutka Bay spot near the high tide rim, looking at the remnants of the hearth hidden within the rock, where we've found small fragments of tools and bone and stone. We feel the power of these women, wishing we could tell them our stories and know theirs. We feel the weight of history here in the sand, and we can almost see women working, almost hear them chattering. Perhaps a thousand years from now, there will still be fish in the ocean, and there will be women standing here cutting fish and laughing together.

Gifts found at Tutka Bay Lodge most often come from the sea, and one beloved treasure is our water grill. We have an area naturally carved from a rock formation that we use as a wood-fired grill during low-tide. During the high tide, the ocean washes the grill to clean and salt it. Sometimes bits of seaweed cling to the grill after being submerged, and we just leave it be for extra flavor. Later, we're going to cook our salmon over alder wood we've gathered from the nearby forest, and we'll have a feast on the beach.

> In discovering our native hearth, we've been led to contemplate those who were here before us.

To start our fire, we find two solid and dry pieces of alder, and we add lighter pieces across the top of those, and then across again, like a foundation of a little log cabin. Next, we spray some oil over dried sedge grass we've bundled into fist-sized balls and stuff these into the base of the fire ring. When the fire is roaring, and then smoldering, we sit on a massive log that washed up years ago after a big storm. It's become a perfect fish prep table, buffet table, and a late-evening hang-out-and-let's-talk bench.

In discovering our native hearth, we've been led again to contemplate those who were here before us. We talk about what it must have been like in Kachemak Bay in the late 1700s when Russians arrived. We talk about what it must have been like for early pioneers trying to carve out a life here, or gold-seekers with big dreams, or hippies in the seventies with world-changing passions. We don't know (at least yet) who the Natives were that built our hearth. Kachemak Bay was a trading place for Athabaskans coming from the Interior, and for Inupiaq traveling far from home, and for Alutiiq who lived along the coast nearby. We don't know how many generations used our hearth before it fell dormant. To understand our little cove and the hearth left behind for us to find, we lean into local Alutiiq/Sugpiaq spirit. A shared respect for salmon and an acceptance of its importance along with the deep sense of love for this land binds us together. Salmon is life in Alaska. Salmon has shaped and fueled and guided our family's direction for more than forty years. Mandy pokes a stick into the fire and turns over a glowing log. It won't be dark here until later in August, months from now, and then we can sit in darkness. For now, we just admire the slant of the sun over the sparkling water, and we watch an old otter float contentedly nearby. This place is his refuge as well as ours.

> Salmon has shaped and fueled and guided our family's direction for more than forty years.

In honor of the Alutiiq people, we have crafted a set of values modeled after their traditional cosmology, a further way to bind us together. It's a living statement of who we are and how we are guided by people from a long distant past.

OUR LAND IS VITAL TO US. We are stewards of several pieces of land in Alaska, and we want these places to be available to others into the future. We are tied to our homeland, to the animals, Earth, sky, and water. Loving this land is a way of being alive. (This is our physical sphere.)

PEOPLE ARE IMPORTANT TO US. The work we do is to care for our guests and bring them into our Alaska lives. We want to show our guests why we live here, what we love about living here. We want to show them the fragile beauty of wild places. (This is our social sphere.)

LEARNING IS ESSENTIAL TO US. We want to continually learn how to do our jobs better, to know more about the natural world where we live, and understand the connectivity of people from the past to present in this place. We want to keep heritage alive and learn old ways of traditional arts and ingenuity. (This is our cognitive sphere.)

SPIRITUAL REFLECTION IS MEANINGFUL FOR US. We want to breathe in the wild, clean air, and capture the beauty of rare and elusive moments as they happen. We want to appreciate the here and now. We want to listen to the past. (This is our spiritual sphere.)

TRUST AND SHARING ARE GOOD FOR US. We welcome and accept all of our guests openly. We want our food to facilitate sharing and communion at the table. We hope to inspire our guests to care about and respect the natural world. (This is our ethical sphere.)

The tide begins to rise and lap over the cove, and our broad, sandy beach starts to disappear underneath waves of water. We splash a bucket of seawater onto the fire and pick up the strips of salmon that have been hanging and smoking overhead. With bowls and plates tucked underarm, we head back to the lodge. Much later, we notice a small silver spoon is missing. Perhaps we've dropped it in the sand near the fire—and, maybe a thousand years from now, someone will wonder about who we were.

WHITEFISH CHILI

We make an effort to use other Alaska fish species beyond salmon, although from reading this book, you can probably tell where our hearts lie. We serve this chili with Camp Bread (page 59) and sour cream. Try making this over live-fire like we do during Girls' Fish Camp day.

MAKES 4 TO 6 SERVINGS

1 tablespoon canola oil

1 poblano chile, diced

1 red bell pepper, julienned

1 yellow bell pepper, julienned

1 large yellow onion, peeled and diced

6 cloves garlic, minced

Sea salt and freshly ground black pepper

1 tablespoon ground cumin

1½ teaspoons ground coriander

1 teaspoon pure chile powder

½ teaspoon red pepper flakes

4 cups stewed diced tomatoes

6 cups store-bought or homemade chicken stock

Juice of 2 limes

3 cups cooked large white beans, drained and rinsed

2 pounds cod or halibut fillet

¼ cup finely chopped fresh cilantro

Leaves from 2 sprigs fresh thyme

Camp Bread (page 59) for serving (optional)

Add the canola oil to a 6-quart casserole and place it over medium-high heat. Add the chile peppers, onion, and garlic and sauté until soft, about 10 minutes. Season lightly with salt and pepper. Add the cumin, coriander, chile powder, and red pepper flakes. Continue to sauté for 1 more minute to toast the spices. Stir in the stewed tomatoes with their liquid, stock, and lime juice and bring to a simmer. Add the beans and continue to simmer for 20 more minutes.

Pat the fish completely dry with paper towels. Cut the fish into 1- to 2-inch cubes. Drop in the fish and cilantro into the chili and continue to simmer until heated through, 5 to 7 minutes. Taste the chili for seasoning and adjust if necessary.

To serve, ladle into bowls and sprinkle with the thyme or put spoonfuls on rounds of Camp Bread.

CAMP BREAD

This is a very basic version of the fry bread people in Alaska have been making forever. Sometimes we add bits of smoked salmon, green onion, sautéed onion, and other ingredients. It's a great outdoor camping bread that is best eaten hot. Here, we give you instructions for making the bread in a home kitchen. We serve these with our Whitefish Chili (page 56).

MAKES 4 TO 6 BREADS

1 cup all-purpose flour, plus more for dusting

½ cup barley flour

2 teaspoons baking powder

2 teaspoons sea salt, plus more for sprinkling

1 teaspoon fresh thyme leaves

1 clove garlic, minced

½ cup buttermilk

¼ cup sour cream

3 cups canola oil, for frying

In a bowl, combine the flours, baking powder, salt, thyme, and garlic. Add the buttermilk and sour cream and mix until a dough forms. Turn the dough out onto a lightly floured work surface and knead for 5 minutes, then transfer to a clean bowl and cover with a clean kitchen towel. Let the dough rest for 10 minutes.

Preheat the oven to 225°F. Line a baking sheet with parchment paper.

Divide the dough into 8 equal portions, pressing down on each to make a flattened disk about ¼-inch thick. Then, pat and roll out the dough balls into roughly 6-inch disks. Cover the dough disks with a clean kitchen towel while you prepare to fry them.

Heat the oil in a 6-quart casserole over medium heat until it reaches around 350°F on a deep-frying thermometer, about 5 minutes. Working in batches, fry the disks in the hot oil until golden brown on one side, then carefully flip with tongs and fry on the other side in the same manner. Set on a paper towel to drain, then transfer to the prepared baking sheet and keep warm in the oven while you fry the rest of the bread.

To serve, sprinkle with a little salt and serve warm.

SHRIMP HONEY PUFFS

We serve these puffs year round, but they are particularly delicious in May and June when the boats come into the harbor with fresh shrimp to sell. We serve them most often at appetizer hour with a crisp, cool white wine.

MAKES ABOUT 24 PUFFS

Canola oil for frying

6 tablespoons unsalted butter

1 cup store-bought or homemade chicken stock

1 tablespoon sea salt, plus more for sprinkling

1½ cups bread flour

4 large eggs

¼ cup grated Parmigiano-Reggiano cheese, plus extra for dusting

Freshly ground black pepper

¼ cup chopped fresh cilantro

½ pound Alaska shrimp, peeled and minced

½ cup honey, warmed

Pour the oil into a casserole or electric deep-fryer until it comes about halfway up the sides. Warm the oil over medium-high heat until it reads 350°F on a deep-frying thermometer.

In a 4-quart saucepan, combine the butter, stock, and salt and bring to a boil. Remove from the heat and add in the bread flour all at once. Using a sturdy wooden spoon, stir until a smooth, shiny dough is formed. Return the pan to the heat and stir constantly until the mixture comes away from the sides of the pan, about 2 minutes. Remove from the heat.

Add in the eggs, one at a time, mixing thoroughly after each addition. Add in the grated cheese, pepper to taste, and the cilantro. Fold in the shrimp to make the dough.

Working in batches, drop the dough by tablespoons into the hot oil and fry until puffy and golden brown, 2 to 3 minutes. Remove the puffs with a wire mesh spoon and drain on paper towels. Sprinkle with salt and additional cheese. Drizzle with the honey and serve hot.

Variation: For baked puffs, put the dough into a pastry bag (you don't need a tip) and pipe into 2-inch balls spaced 1 inch apart onto a parchment-lined baking sheet. Bake in a preheated 400°F oven for 10 minutes. Reduce the heat to 325°F and continue to bake until golden brown, 10 to 15 minutes (this will vary depending on how large or small your puffs are). Sprinkle with sea salt and additional cheese before serving.

FIRE-ROASTED FISH COLLARS

Exemplifying our "Waste Not" philosophy, we usually work with whole fish in our kitchens, rather than already cut fillets, and we have plenty of carcasses and fish parts that many people just toss away. We aim to use as much of a fish as we possibly can. Fish collars are meaty and fatty and pretty delicious, even if they are a bit hard to eat with any sort of dainty manners. If you are able to grill outside over live fire, this is the best. We use alder wood, but other aromatic woods work too.

MAKES 4 SERVINGS

1-inch knob ginger, peeled
   and thinly sliced

1 fresh bird's eye chile, minced

2 cloves garlic, minced

1 cup water

½ cup soy sauce

½ cup sake

½ cup honey

4 salmon collars (about 3 pounds total),
   scaled, fins removed

Canola oil for the grill

Sea salt and freshly ground black pepper

Make a marinade: in a saucepan over medium heat, bring the ginger, chile, garlic, water, soy sauce, sake, and honey to a boil. Reduce the heat to low and simmer, stirring occasionally, until the liquid is reduced by half, about 10 minutes. Let the marinade cool. Set aside about ½ cup of the marinade.

Pour the remaining marinade into a glass or ceramic bowl. Add the salmon collars and turn them to coat completely with the marinade. Cover the bowl with a kitchen towel or Bee's Wrap. Chill in the refrigerator for about 1 hour.

If you are grilling the salmon, prepare a medium-hot fire in a wood- or charcoal-fired grill and set a grate over the fire that has been well oiled with canola oil. Remove the salmon from the marinade. Place the salmon on the grill grate skin-side down, and grill until the skin is lacquered and brown, brushing occasionally with reserved marinade, 3 to 6 minutes, depending on how hot your fire is. Repeat on the other side of the fish. (It should only take about 10 minutes total to cook the fish.)

If you are roasting the salmon, preheat the oven to 350°F. Remove the salmon from the marinade. Place the salmon collars onto a parchment-lined baking sheet. Bake until the skin is lacquered and brown, brushing the collars occasionally with some of the leftover marinade, 3 to 6 minutes on each side.

Serve hot.

WATER GRILL OYSTERS

We have a cluster of rocks at Tutka Bay Lodge that we use for a grill site. We place a meshed grill grate over an alder wood fire and cook shellfish, such as these oysters, right on the beach. When the tide comes in, it washes away the grill site and salts it with sea water, ready for the next beach cookout.

MAKES 8 TO 12 SERVINGS

1 cup plus 2 tablespoons unsalted butter, softened

2 tablespoons white miso

½ cup seaweed flakes

1 tablespoon sake

2 cloves garlic, finely minced

1 small shallot, finely minced

1 cup panko breadcrumbs

Sea salt and freshly ground black pepper

1 tablespoon chopped fresh chives

3 tablespoons finely grated Parmigiano-Reggiano cheese

2 dozen oysters, cleaned and unshucked

In a bowl, mix 1 cup butter, the miso, seaweed flakes, sake, garlic, and shallot until well blended. Place a sheet of parchment paper on a work surface. Using a rubber spatula, spread the mixture near the edge of the paper. Then, roll the butter mixture in the parchment to form a cylinder about 1 inch thick. Seal the cylinder with a piece of tape. Refrigerate the butter until firm, about 20 minutes. Once firm, remove the butter from the parchment and slice it into 24 rounds. Keep chilled until ready to use.

In a saucepan over medium heat, melt the 2 tablespoons butter until just foaming. Add the panko and toss to coat. Season to taste with salt and pepper. Toast the panko until light golden brown, 1 to 2 minutes. Remove from the heat. Add the chives and cheese and toss to mix. Set aside.

Prepare a medium-hot fire in a grill. When the grill is ready, place oysters directly on the grill grate, flat side up. Cover the grill and cook until the oyster shells just pop open, 3 to 4 minutes. Transfer the oysters to a baking sheet, discarding any that failed to open up.

Using tongs or your fingers, pull off the flat side of each oyster shell. Use an oyster knife to cut under the muscle to free the oyster and leave it in the cupped shell; try to keep the oyster liquor in the shell. Place 1 round of butter onto each cooked oyster and top each with 2 teaspoons of the breadcrumb mixture. Carefully return the oysters to the grill and cover.

Cook the oysters until the topping is slightly caramelized and sizzling, 2 to 3 minutes. Serve immediately.

MUSSELS ROASTED OVER SPRUCE BOUGHS

This is a technique we learned in France. We arrange the mussels in a pretty pattern on the beach and cover them in spruce and dead beach grass. Then, as we gather around the bonfire, we take a burning stick and ignite the covered mussels to roast them open, then drizzle them with a little garlic butter. These are delicious with sourdough toast on the side, and they go great with a local IPA beer. Eat the mussels right off the grill or serve on a bed of charred spruce.

MAKES 4 LARGE SERVINGS

1 pound unsalted butter

4 cloves garlic, minced

2 teaspoons finely grated lemon zest

8 sprigs fresh tarragon, finely chopped

1 teaspoon chemical- and pesticide-free spruce tips, minced

1 teaspoon sea salt

4 small spruce boughs, enough to cover the grill surface and some to cover mussels

Dried seagrass or straw, if desired

4 pounds fresh mussels, scrubbed and debearded

In a small saucepan, melt the butter. Add the garlic, lemon zest, tarragon, spruce tips, and salt. Whisk to combine and set aside.

Prepare a medium-hot fire in a grill. Place the spruce boughs over the fire. As soon as the spruce boughs begins to sizzle and release wisps of steam and smoke, place the mussels directly over the boughs and cover with more spruce and dried grass, if using. Cover the grill. The spruce will smolder and smoke as the mussels pop open. Uncover the grill and check them at about 10 minutes. Use tongs to remove the opened mussels from the grill and place them on a heatproof platter. Cook stubborn mussels for a few minutes longer in the covered grill; if they don't open after about 5 minutes, discard the unopened mussels.

Drizzle some garlic-herb butter over the mussels on the platter and serve with additional butter for dipping.

SMOKED & SALTED CARAMEL BLUEBERRY BROWNIE

These brownies offer the combination of smoky caramel, blueberries, and chocolate. Throw in walnuts if you like. Here's our special way to serve the brownies: We wrap the cut bars in individual birch bark boats and tie with twine. Then, we bring them to our camp site and, after cooking dinner over the campfire, we place the packages directly onto smoldering coals and cover with a tent of foil. We smoke the brownies for 1 to 2 minutes, depending on how smoky the fire is, then remove them and serve with hot coffee.

MAKES 24 BROWNIES

2 cups unsalted butter, cubed, plus more for greasing

2½ cups all-purpose flour

1 cup unsweetened cocoa powder

2 teaspoons sea salt

1½ teaspoons baking powder

1 pound dark chocolate chunks

10 large eggs, at room temperature

3 cups granulated sugar

1 cup packed light brown sugar

1 tablespoon pure vanilla bean paste or vanilla extract

½ cup whole milk, at room temperature

1½ cups fresh blueberries or frozen, drained blueberries

6 ounces semisweet chocolate chips

Smoked, Salted Caramel Sauce (page 288), cooled slightly

Smoked sea salt, for sprinkling

Line a 13-by-8-inch rimmed baking sheet with parchment paper and butter the pan and sides well. Preheat the oven to 350°F.

In a bowl, whisk together the flour, cocoa, salt, and baking power. In a heatproof bowl placed over a pot of simmering water, melt the butter cubes with the dark chocolate chunks. Stir until the mixture is smooth.

In the bowl of a mixer fitted with the whisk attachment, beat the eggs and both sugars on medium speed until the mixture is pale in color and when you lift the whisk the batter falls slowly in a ribbon and holds its shape, about 5 minutes. Add the vanilla paste and mix well. On the lowest mixer speed, whisk in the flour mixture along with the butter-chocolate mixture, alternating with the milk. Stir until just combined. Fold in the blueberries and semisweet chocolate chips.

Pour the mixture into the prepared baking sheet. Using a small ice cream scoop, place 8 scoops of caramel sauce on top of the batter, spacing them out evenly. Take a butter knife or small off-set spatula and swirl the caramel sauce around the brownie batter. Finish with a sprinkle of smoked salt on top.

Bake until a cake tester inserted into the center of the brownie comes out clean, about 30 minutes. Remove the pan from the oven and let the brownie cool completely on a wire rack.

To serve, cut the brownies into approximately 2-by-4-inch bars.

BLACK COD WITH MUSHROOM CARAMEL SAUCE

Black cod, also called butterfish or sablefish, has the ability to take on flavors and make them taste even better. The fish's loose muscle bands always make for crispy edges. Serve this rich combination with simple white rice and a steamed vegetable. We source our black cod right in Kachemak Bay, where our Tutka Bay Lodge is located.

MAKES 4 SERVINGS

⅔ cup apple cider vinegar

⅓ cup water

½ cup dried domestic mushrooms

1 cup sugar

1 cup honey

½ cup whiskey

½ cup heavy cream

1 teaspoon sea salt, plus more as needed

4 (4-ounce) black cod fillets, skinned

Freshly ground black pepper

In a small saucepan over medium heat, combine the vinegar and water, heating just until the mixture boils. Add the mushrooms, turn off the heat, and let the mixture stand for a few minutes until soft. Strain the mushrooms through a fine-mesh sieve, reserving the liquid.

In the same saucepan, combine the mushroom liquid, sugar, and honey. Heat on low until the color changes to a light amber, 8 to 10 minutes. Be sure you turn on your kitchen ventilation. Add the whiskey and carefully use a match to ignite the mixture and let the alcohol burn off. Remove the pan from the heat and add the cream. Whisk until combined.

Return the mushrooms to the pan and add 1 teaspoon salt. If the mixture seems too liquidy, simmer over low heat to thicken it. If it seems too thick, add warm water to thin it. Set the sauce aside.

Turn on your oven's broiler to low. Line a baking sheet with aluminum foil.

Pat the fillets completely dry and season lightly with salt and pepper. Place the fillets onto the foil-lined baking sheet and baste well with some of the sauce.

Broil the fish about 6 inches away from the heat source until the fish is just cooked in the center, 4 to 5 minutes. Remove the cod from the oven and baste with any extra sauce. Serve warm.

FIRST OF THE YEAR SALMON SOUP

This soup celebrates the first salmon returning to our rivers in the springtime—it's a high energy moment when they arrive. This soup is simple so you can make it quickly in your kitchen or on the beach. We tend to use chicken stock with fish soups to balance the flavor. And, we love to use miso, which goes so naturally with our Alaskan fish. We honor our salmon by always using every bit we can. We scrape meat from the leftover salmon carcasses and add it to our soup.

MAKES 4 SERVINGS

6 ounces extra-firm tofu

5-inch piece of kombu seaweed

6 cups store-bought or homemade chicken stock

6 fresh shiitake mushrooms, stemmed and sliced

2 cloves garlic, thinly sliced

8 ounces salmon scrap meat

2 tablespoons white miso

2 green onions, minced

Cut the tofu into ½-inch cubes. Tear the sea lettuce into 1-inch pieces.

In a 6-quart casserole, bring the stock to a boil over medium heat. Add the mushrooms, tofu, kombu, and garlic. Reduce the heat and simmer for 2 to 3 minutes, to develop the flavors. Add the salmon and miso. Gently simmer until the salmon is just cooked through, about 5 minutes.

Ladle the soup into serving bowls and serve hot garnished with the green onions.

BEER-BATTERED COD CAKES

This is a different take on "fish and chips," featuring a fish cake that we serve at lunch with a beautiful salad or at bar appetizer hour with a collection of dips. We always keep the trim when we're butchering pieces of fish such as cod, halibut, and salmon. Then, we make cakes from these smaller pieces of fish and never waste a bit. We use shrimp to bind the cakes rather than eggs or crackers.

MAKES 4 TO 5 SERVINGS

6 peppercorns

1 bay leaf

1 lemon, quartered

1 pound boneless and skinless
  cod pieces, rinsed and patted dry

2 tablespoons unsalted butter

½ yellow onion, diced

1 clove garlic, minced

¼ pound Alaska shrimp,
  peeled and chopped

½ bunch fresh flat-leaf parsley,
  roughly chopped

¼ teaspoon sea salt

1 quart canola oil, for frying

1½ cups all-purpose flour

1 teaspoon curry powder

1 cup IPA-style beer

2 egg whites, whipped to soft peaks

Tartar sauce or Rhubarb Chutney
  (page 291) for dipping

Fill a high-sided saucepan with 2 inches of water and set over high heat. Add the peppercorns, bay leaf, and 2 lemon quarters and bring to a simmer. Place the cod into the liquid and cook, barely simmering, until the flesh has just begun to whiten, 5 to 7 minutes, depending on the thickness of the fish. Transfer the cod to paper towels to drain.

Empty the saucepan and return it to medium-high heat. Add the butter, onion, and garlic, and sauté until the onion turns translucent, 5 to 7 minutes. Transfer to a bowl and let cool.

Place the cooked cod, shrimp, cooled onion mixture, parsley, and salt into a food processor. Pulse the mixture several times to combine. Transfer the mixture to a bowl and refrigerate for about 30 minutes to firm up.

Dipping your hands into a bowl of cold water, form the fish mixture into 2-ounce balls (about 2 inches in diameter).

Pour the canola oil into a heavy 4-quart casserole or deep-fryer and warm over medium-high heat until it reads 350°F on a deep-frying thermometer.

In a bowl, mix together 1 cup of the flour, the curry powder, and the beer. Fold in the egg whites to make a batter. Place the remaining ½ cup flour onto a small plate. One at a time, slightly flatten a fish ball and dredge it in the flour, shaking off the excess, then dip into the beer batter, then ease into the hot oil. Fry the fish cakes until they puff and turn light golden brown, 6 to 8 minutes. Transfer the fish cakes to paper towels to drain. Serve warm.

TUTKA BAY FISH STEW

Of all the variations on fish stew, soup, and chowder, this is Kirsten's favorite. There's a definite Spanish vibe with the addition of almonds to the stew. In our cooking classes, we teach students to grate the tomatoes on the large holes of a cheese grater for ease.

MAKES 4 SERVINGS

½ cup extra-virgin olive oil

2 cloves garlic, sliced

¼ cup blanched almonds

Leaves from 1 bunch flat-leaf parsley

1 teaspoon smoked paprika

6 cups plus 2 tablespoons store-bought or homemade chicken stock

Sea salt

8 red fingerling potatoes

1 yellow onion, diced

4 tomatoes, grated or diced

Pinch of saffron threads

1 sprig fresh thyme

1 bay leaf

½ cup sparkling white wine

2 pounds cod fillet, cut into small pieces

1 pound halibut fillet, cut into small pieces

In a small sauté pan, warm 2 tablespoons of the oil over medium heat. Add the garlic and sauté until aromatic and translucent, 1 to 2 minutes. Let the garlic and oil cool slightly and then pour into a blender. Add the almonds, parsley, paprika, and 2 tablespoons chicken stock and blend until a paste forms. Season to taste with salt. Set aside.

In a large saucepan over medium heat, warm the remaining 6 tablespoons of the oil. Add the potatoes and onion and sauté until the onions are translucent, 5 to 7 minutes. Add the grated tomatoes and saffron and sauté for a few minutes longer. Add the thyme and bay leaf. Pour in the wine and sauté for a few minutes until the alcohol cooks off. Then, add the remaining 6 cups chicken stock. Bring the liquid to a light simmer.

Add the cod and halibut to the slowly simmering broth (adjust the heat if necessary) and cook until the potatoes are tender and the fish is cooked through, 10 to 12 minutes. Remove the bay leaf.

Season the stew to taste with salt. Stir in the garlic-almond mixture and cook until the flavors are combined, about 5 more minutes.

Ladle the stew into bowls and serve hot.

A CUISINE OF OUR OWN

Our personalized northern kingdom lies between the coastlines and uplands of the central Gulf of Alaska, with Tutka Bay Lodge and the café to the south of Anchorage and Winterlake Lodge to the north. In the geographic sense, and sometimes in the emotional sense, the city of Anchorage is the anchor between our two facets of coastal and mountain life.

These days, despite having our own rooms at the lodges and an apartment on the Homer Spit, Kirsten has a small house, and Mandy has a condo in Anchorage that gives us something of a reverse refuge from our day-to-day world, our own version of weekend getaway cabins. We can come "to town" and take long, hot showers, be totally quiet and private in our personal spaces, and not have to worry about the woodstove or the animals or all the other lodge chores. Anchorage offers us all the worldly sophistication we need such as art, libraries, and bookstores. But, best of all, Anchorage is growing in culinary diversity. We have some of the best Asian, particularly Korean, markets anywhere. And Anchorage's farmer markets display a wide range of culinary delicacies from baked bread to black tomatoes. So, as the world gets smaller and comes to us, how do we define a cuisine of our own with a distinctive sense of place?

Popular foods in Alaska tell the story of our cultural, political, and natural past—and present. Just look at the onion domes on some churches, Russian Orthodox slanted crosses, and remnants of old Russian tsarist dialect found in villages near Tutka Bay, and you can easily find imprints of Russia's eighty-three years of colonialism in Alaska. It's the same with food that is now considered "traditional" in some old Alaska family repertoires. Salmon pie, cabbage dishes, beets in soup and salads, all speak to people who came here from Russia. Russian cuisine is an integral part of our culinary story.

Other visitors to Alaska also came here to find their fortunes. Scandinavians came to fish and to seek gold. There's a high proportion of Norwegian and Danish people who made their way here during the wild gold rush and commercial fishing days. We particularly weave Danish food into our cuisine since we have a Danish family heritage. One of the classes we teach at our cooking school is a Danish family recipe for, well, Danishes. In Denmark, these buttery pastries are called Vienerbrod, or Vienna bread. In 1850, there was a strike amongst bakery workers, and so quite a few Austrian bakers were imported to relieve the shortage. They came making the soft dough pastries that they learned from invading Turks. (It's interesting how many regional foods are born of war.) In our Danish recipe, we always use cardamom, an exotic East Indian spice that has, through travel and trade, become emblematic of Scandinavian cooking.

> Anchorage offers us all the worldly sophistication we need...

Asian food also influences our cooking. We are the closest U.S. port to both China and Japan, places we have both traveled to. Japanese culinary aesthetic fits in comfortably with our simple and seasonal cooking. And, Chinese food culture emphasizes generosity and communal abundance at the table. We've somehow in our family adopted Chinese New Year as a favorite food tradition—with noodles, red lanterns, and all.

We make an effort to learn about the people who may have come before us. We search out native Alaska stories about foodways and traditions, like the history of Mary Antisarlook. Known as Sinrock Mary, she worked as a translator for Michael Healy, a boat captain who brought reindeer to Alaska from Siberia and, later, Lapland. Mary faced many obstacles of race and gender in her life. When Mary's husband died, her brothers-in-law took her house and money but allowed her to keep a small portion of her husband's reindeer herd. She built up her herd, and, through a keen business sense, she sold reindeer meat to gold miners and soldiers. She became the richest woman in Alaska.

Alaska's Native culture is always with us as we think about what Alaska food culture means to us. We weave Native stories of the past as we can into our menus. We learn from elders about wild plants, and how to forage, how to smoke and preserve salmon, and how to make bread over a live fire.

> Alaska's Native culture is always with us as we think about what Alaska food culture means to us.

And, we admire those hearty souls who trudged through muck and hardship at the turn of the last century to find their fortunes in gold. Beans, bacon, sourdough, and all the other foods of a lost era are still on our minds. A knock on the door can reveal a frozen-cold traveler standing in the doorway. We give them beans and sourdough bread at the table to warm them up! Sometimes we feel like we have an old bygone roadhouse at Winterlake Lodge when people start traveling the Iditarod Trail in winter. It's not far off to think this. In the late 1800s, there was a roadhouse every twenty miles along the Iditarod Trail. That's the distance a dog team could reasonably travel in a day. Some roadhouses were famous for delicious food, warm hospitality, and clean accommodations. Others were filthy, and the food was distasteful. It's a choice people have always made, whether to live well within their circumstances or not. Most of the old roadhouse sites between Winterlake Lodge and the village of McGrath, another Iditarod checkpoint, are gone now, either sunk into the ground or washed away by river erosion. There is an uncorroborated story that a roadhouse closest to our present-day lodge was run by a Japanese man who made the most incredible sourdough pancakes. It doesn't hurt us to help a weary traveler from time to time, in the tradition of old roadhouses, and, in some way, we are carrying on an old and noble Alaska lifestyle.

Imagine the stories of adventure, love lost and won, and fortunes found and squandered during the Alaska gold-rush era. There were hard-working women cooking in roadhouses and tent-camps throughout it all, and later on, proper little cafés if they were lucky, feeding wild and rugged gold seekers. There's a statue in the town of Skagway of a young woman named Molly Walsh that captivates our imagination. Commissioned by one of her café regulars, the inscription reads, "Alone and with help, this courageous girl ran a grub tent near Log Cabin during the Gold Rush of 1897–1898. She fed and lodged the wildest gold-crazed men. Generations shall surely know this inspiring spirit. Murdered October 27, 1902."

The echoes of Sinrock Mary and Molly Walsh; of our Danish grandmothers baking pastries given to Austrians by invading Turks; courageous explorers from Japan, China, and Scandinavia; have all laid a foundation for our Alaska culinary history. These often heartbreaking and sometimes beautifully romantic stories of tough and hearty, colorful, and full-of-life people swirl around us as we cook in our kitchens. The old stories inspire us to remember those people who have come before us. That's Alaska cuisine.

SALMON HAND PIES

These little handheld pies have been in our family repertoire ever since Kirsten would make them for Carl as he worked on our log lodge during the day and wouldn't stop for lunch. Hand pies are found in almost every cuisine around the world. There are plenty of variations out there, but try our version first!

MAKES SIX 4-INCH HAND PIES

3 tablespoons unsalted butter, plus more if needed

1 small red onion, minced

½ pound domestic mushrooms, cleaned and sliced

½ head green cabbage, cored and shredded

1 pound salmon, skinned and boned

1 teaspoon canola oil

Sea salt and freshly ground black pepper

2 sheets Homemade Puff Pastry (page 291) or store-bought all-butter puff pastry

All-purpose flour

2 cups cooked short-grain brown rice

1 hard-boiled egg, chopped

½ cup shredded Manchego cheese

½ cup fine breadcrumbs

1 tablespoon minced fresh flat-leaf parsley

¼ cup heavy cream

1 egg, beaten

Preheat the oven to 375°F. Have ready six 4-inch ring molds.

Melt the butter in a wide sauté pan over low heat. Add the onion and sauté until soft, about 7 minutes. (The lower the heat over which the onion cooks, the less likely it is to burn.) Add the mushrooms and cabbage. Turn the heat up to medium, adding a bit more butter if necessary, and stir everything together. Place a lid or a piece of foil over the cabbage-vegetable mixture to hold in the steam and cook until the cabbage and mushrooms are tender, 5 to 7 minutes. Transfer the vegetables to a plate or bowl and set aside.

Cut the salmon into 1-inch cubes. Add the oil to a nonstick sauté pan, and place over medium heat. When the oil is hot, add the salmon cubes and sear on all sides until the fish is cooked through, about 4 minutes. Season with salt and

pepper to taste. Cool the salmon slightly and flake it into small pieces with your fingers.

Line a standard baking sheet with parchment paper and set aside. Place the puff pastry on a floured work surface. Using a rolling pin, roll out the puff pastry until ⅛ inch thick, which will help prevent it from puffing too much during baking. We like to use a good sturdy rolling pin that has some weight and width to it. Using a 6-inch cutter or a cleaned, empty can or jar that is about 2 inches larger in diameter than the ring molds, cut the puff pastry into 12 rounds. Place the ring molds, evenly spaced, onto the prepared baking sheet. Place 1 puff pastry round on top of each ring mold. Press the dough down in the ring mold to make a well, making sure the dough drapes over the sides of the mold.

Divide the brown rice evenly among the ring molds on top of the pastry rounds. Press down lightly to make an even layer. Next, sprinkle in the chopped hard-boiled egg, dividing evenly. Add a layer of flaked salmon, then some grated cheese into the molds, again dividing evenly. Next add the breadcrumbs and parsley. Finally, divide the onion, mushroom, and cabbage mixture among the ring molds. Sprinkle the filling of each pie with salt and pepper to taste. Pour a small amount of the heavy cream over the filling ingredients.

Brush the rim of the pastry with a little water. Place a second pastry round on top of the filling, lining up the edges. Trim off the excess dough but leave enough to crimp the edges of the pie together to adhere the two sheets of dough. Some people do this with a fork or between 2 fingers to make a decorative edge. Slit the pie top with a few knife slashes so that steam can escape. Brush the top of the pie with the beaten egg. Repeat to make 5 more hand pies. Remove the ring molds.

Bake the pies until the pastry is golden brown and the filling is warmed through, 35 to 40 minutes.

Serve warm or at room temperature.

PICKLED SALMON BELLY

When butchering whole salmon, we trim the belly meat from the fillets to have uniform pieces for searing. But the belly meat is not to be wasted—it is rich in fat and flavor. We love to fry these up in a pan of butter or make rillettes from the deeply colored flesh, but sometimes we have too many and need to preserve them. Pickled salmon is delicious on a cracker with a little cheese and white wine.

MAKES 2 POUNDS PICKLED SALMON

FOR THE PICKLING LIQUID

1 cup water

3 cups rice vinegar

2 bay leaves, crumbled

2 teaspoons black peppercorns

½ cup sugar

¼ cup sea salt

2 tablespoons whole mustard seeds

2 teaspoons whole coriander seeds

1 teaspoon whole allspice

1 teaspoon red pepper flakes

½-inch knob ginger, peeled and grated

2 pounds salmon bellies, skin scraped off

6 shallots, sliced into thin rounds

2 lemons, sliced into thin rounds

To make the pickling liquid, in a saucepan, combine the water, vinegar, bay leaves, peppercorns, sugar, and salt and bring to a boil over high heat. When the mixture comes to a boil, turn off the heat and add the mustard seeds, coriander seeds, allspice, red pepper flakes, and ginger. Set aside to steep and let the liquid cool completely.

Cut the salmon belly into ½-inch pieces. In a large, sterilized canning jar or several small canning jars, layer the salmon alternating with layers of shallot and lemon. Pour the cooled liquid over the salmon, submerging the salmon completely. Cover the jar(s) securely and refrigerate for 3 days or until ready to use.

DEEP PURPLE SALAD WITH KALE & BERRIES

There are so many shades of purple growing in our gardens, we decided to make a salad celebrating them. Serve this with crisp, skin-side-up sockeye salmon or as a lovely vegetarian luncheon.

MAKES 6 MAIN-DISH OR 12 SIDE-DISH SERVINGS

4 cups chopped red cabbage

1 tablespoon sugar

1 teaspoon sea salt

2 cups fresh spinach, stemmed

1 bunch red kale, stemmed and chopped

1 bunch red Swiss chard, stemmed and chopped

4 cooked small red beets, diced

1 cup dried red currants or dried cranberries

2 cups fresh blueberries

1 cup shelled sunflower seeds, toasted

FOR THE DRESSING

½ cup Blueberry Syrup (page 287)

1 tablespoon honey

¼ cup apple cider vinegar

Sea salt and freshly ground black pepper

¾ cup canola oil

½ cup dried beet chips

Place the red cabbage into a large bowl. Sprinkle the cabbage with the sugar and salt, then use your hands to massage the cabbage to break it down a bit and release some of its liquid. Add the spinach, kale, chard, beets, currants, and blueberries and gently toss. Add the sunflower seeds and gently toss. Set aside while you make the dressing.

To make the dressing, whisk together the syrup, honey, and vinegar. Add salt and pepper to taste. While whisking, drizzle in the oil to lightly blend the ingredients. (This dressing will be a broken dressing, not an emulsified one.)

Pour the dressing over the salad and toss together. Garnish with the beet chips. Serve right away.

KHYCHINY (RUSSIAN FLATBREADS)

We discovered these delicious breads, sold by local Russian women, at our Homer Farmers Market. Fillings can be endless with this interesting dough. We like to cook the breads on our outdoor grill, but you can bake them in the oven just as well. Our guests love to enjoy these out on the deck at appetizer time.

MAKES 12 SMALL FLATBREADS

FOR THE DOUGH

2¼ cups buttermilk

3 teaspoons active dry yeast

1 teaspoon sugar

4 tablespoons unsalted butter, melted and cooled, plus butter for the bowl

3 teaspoons sea salt

6 cups all-purpose flour, plus more for dusting

FOR THE FILLING

6 small red "B" potatoes, cleaned

Sea salt and freshly ground black pepper

2 tablespoons unsalted butter

2 cloves garlic, minced

1 leek, cleaned and chopped

2¼ cups shredded Manchego cheese

½ bunch fresh mint, chopped

½ cup unsalted butter, melted

Medium-grain sea salt for sprinkling

To make the dough, warm 1 cup of the buttermilk in a small saucepan until it reads 105°F on an instant-read thermometer. In a bowl, stir together the warmed buttermilk, yeast, and sugar. Set aside until the mixture is bubbling, about 5 minutes.

Add the remaining 1¼ cups of the buttermilk, the melted butter, salt, and flour to the buttermilk-yeast mixture and use a wooden spoon to mix well until a rough dough forms. Turn the dough out onto a lightly floured work surface and knead by hand until the dough is smooth and elastic, about 10 minutes.

Transfer the dough to a buttered bowl, cover with a clean kitchen towel, and let rise in a warm place until the dough has doubled in size, about 45 minutes.

Transfer the dough to a floured work surface. Use a large knife or bench scraper to divide the dough into 12 equal pieces. Form each piece into a ball and let rest on the floured work surface, covered with a kitchen towel, while you make the filling.

To make the filling, boil the potatoes in salted water until fork-tender, about 20 minutes. Drain the potatoes through a colander and set aside.

In a sauté pan over medium heat, melt the butter. Add the garlic and leek and sauté until translucent and soft, about 5 minutes.

Continued on page 92

...CONTINUED
KHYCHINY (RUSSIAN FLATBREADS)

To a bowl, add the potatoes and mash them with a fork. Add the cooked leek-garlic mixture, the shredded cheese, and chopped mint. Mix well. Season to taste with salt and pepper.

Prepare a medium-hot fire in a charcoal grill. (Alternatively, preheat the oven to 350°F.) Line a large, rimmed baking sheet with parchment.

Place one of the dough balls onto a lightly floured work surface and gently roll out with a rolling pin into a round about ¼-inch thick. Repeat with the remaining dough rounds, arranging them on the work surface. Divide the filling equally between the dough rounds. Working with one dough round at a time, pull the edges of the dough up and around to encase the filling. Pinch the dough to seal in the filling. At this point they will look like small purses. Sprinkle the dough balls with a bit of flour and

roll the dough out with the filling in the center until about ½-inch thick. Place the finished disks on the prepared baking sheet. Brush the dough with the melted butter and sprinkle with medium-grain sea salt.

Place the dough rounds on the grill grate. Grill until the dough starts to color and bubble, about 2 minutes, then, flip the dough and cook until the other side is golden brown, about 2 minutes more. Make sure the filling is hot and the cheese is melted. (Alternatively, bake the dough rounds in the preheated oven until golden brown, 15 to 20 minutes.)

Serve hot, right off the grill.

HALIBUT KATSU SANDWICHES

Katsu is short for "katsuretsu" in Japanese, which means cutlet. We sometimes serve halibut cutlets on top of our rice and vegetable bowl specials but, as sandwiches, they are always served on white bread, Japanese style (we love Japanese katsu sandwiches of all types). This is the lunch special on Saturdays at the café and it is always a big hit.

MAKES 4 SERVINGS

FOR THE CABBAGE SALAD
1 cup shredded green cabbage
Sea salt and freshly ground black pepper
2 tablespoons rice vinegar
1 tablespoon canola oil
½ teaspoon sugar

FOR THE KATSU SAUCE
3 tablespoons ketchup
1 tablespoon Worcestershire sauce
1 tablespoon soy sauce
2 teaspoons oyster sauce
1 teaspoon superfine sugar

1 tablespoon plus 1 teaspoon canola oil
1 cup panko breadcrumbs
½ cup sliced yellow onion
1 tablespoon water
1 pound skinless halibut fillet
Sea salt and freshly ground black pepper
½ cup all-purpose flour
2 large eggs
8 slices white bread
½ cup mayonnaise

Preheat the oven to 400°F. Line a baking sheet with parchment paper. Brush the parchment paper lightly with some canola oil.

To prepare the cabbage salad, place the cabbage in a bowl. Sprinkle the cabbage with 1 teaspoon salt and massage the cabbage with your hands for about 1 minute. This helps to tenderize the cabbage and draw out some moisture. Let stand for 5 minutes, then drain the excess liquid from the bowl. Add the vinegar, canola oil, and the sugar and mix well. Adjust the seasonings to taste with additional salt and pepper if needed. Set aside to let the flavors develop.

To prepare the katsu sauce, in a small bowl, whisk together the ketchup, Worcestershire sauce, soy sauce, oyster sauce, and sugar. Set aside.

In a large nonstick skillet, heat 1 tablespoon canola oil over medium-low heat. Add the panko and sauté, stirring often, or until golden, 2 to 3 minutes. Transfer to a paper towel-lined plate and let cool.

Heat a small sauté pan over medium heat. Add 1 teaspoon oil and the sliced onion. Drizzle 1 tablespoon of the Katsu Sauce over the onion, then add the water. Cover the pan and reduce the heat to low and steam the onions until they are tender, about 7 minutes.

Cut the halibut into 4 cutlets, each about 1 inch thick. Pat the halibut with a clean dry towel to remove excess moisture. Season lightly with salt and pepper.

Continued on page 94

...CONTINUED
HALIBUT KATSU SANDWICHES

Set up a breading station: Place the flour in 1 bowl, the prepared panko breadcrumbs in a second bowl, and the eggs into a third bowl. Whisk the eggs until they are well combined. Dredge the fish through the flour to coat it, shaking off the excess. Next, dip the floured fish into the beaten egg until coated, letting the excess drip back into the bowl. Then, dip the coated fish into the panko breadcrumbs so that it is covered on all sides. Press gently with your hands to secure the breadcrumbs to the fish. Place the breaded fish onto a nonstick wire rack and allow the coating to dry for about 15 minutes.

Place the rack with the breaded fish onto a nonstick baking sheet. Bake the breaded fish in the preheated oven until firm to touch, 8 to 10 minutes, depending on the size of the cutlet. Remove the fish from the oven.

To assemble the sandwiches, smear each slice of bread with 1 tablespoon of the mayonnaise and then with some of the katsu sauce. Spread some of the cabbage salad on 4 of the bread slices. Place 1 halibut katsu on top of the cabbage and cover it with additional cabbage salad. Cover each sandwich with 1 of the remaining pieces of bread and press lightly. Cut the sandwiches in half and serve right away.

BREAKFAST RAMEN

We love to cook for the kid in our family, Carly's son, Rohnen Potgieter. He's a good little eater. He will slurp down noodles with the best of them. This is a breakfast dish created for a kid, but we love it too. It is a big hit at the café as well. We make our own ramen noodles, but you can simplify the recipe using store-bought noodles. Don't skimp on the quantity of noodles you serve per person. This is great with our Roasted Vegetable Ramen Broth (see page 292).

MAKES 4 SERVINGS

8 strips good-quality bacon

2 teaspoons unsalted butter

4 large eggs

4 cups store-bought or homemade chicken stock

3 (3-ounce) packages store-bought dry ramen noodles (discard the seasoning packets)

1 teaspoon toasted sesame oil

1 cup shredded cheddar cheese

1 green onion, sliced

½ cup shredded nori

Preheat the oven to 400°F.

Lay the bacon in a single layer on a nonstick or parchment-lined baking sheet. Place the bacon in the oven and bake until the bacon is crispy, about 18 minutes. Drain the bacon on paper towels. When cool, break the bacon into small bits. Set aside.

In a nonstick 7-inch sauté pan, melt 1 teaspoon of the butter over medium heat. Fry each of the four eggs one at a time over easy (we fry them one at a time to keep the nice shape and spread of the egg white): First, crack the egg into the pan, and cook until the white is just set. Flip the egg over and cook for another 20 seconds. Transfer to a plate and keep warm. Repeat with the remaining eggs.

In a saucepan over medium heat, bring the chicken stock to a boil. When the stock is boiling, drop in the ramen noodles. Cook until the noodles are tender, about 3 minutes. Drain the noodles through a colander, saving the stock and returning it to the pan. Put the noodles in a clean bowl and stir in the sesame oil to prevent the noodles from sticking.

Warm the reserved chicken stock over medium heat until simmering. Divide the noodles among 4 wide, Chinese-style noodle bowls. Add the bacon, dividing evenly. Divide the cheese among the bowls. Pour a tablespoon or so of the stock over each bowl of noodles. This is a dry dish, not a soup, so don't put in too much stock. Place one egg on top of each dish. Garnish with the green onion and nori and serve right away.

BELUGA LENTIL CAVIAR ON BLINI

There's no reason why you can't have an elegant dinner party with interesting appetizers in your snowed-in cabin! On those occasions, we turn to lentils, which are a staple in our pantry. They are stored dry and can last forever. We love to serve these elegant snacks at the bar along with salmon caviar as an alternative.

MAKES 6 TO 8 SERVINGS

FOR THE CAVIAR

½ cup black beluga lentils, rinsed and sorted

2 cups water

2 teaspoons sea salt

4-inch sheet of kombu seaweed

1 clove garlic

2 tablespoons minced brine-packed capers

2 tablespoons brine from the caper jar

1 tablespoon extra-virgin olive oil (optional)

FOR THE BLINI BATTER

1 cup lukewarm milk

1 teaspoons active dry yeast

1½ cups all-purpose flour

1 teaspoon sugar

1 teaspoons sea salt

2 large eggs, separated into whites and yolks

¼ cup canola oil

1 tablespoon chopped fresh chives, plus more for garnish

½ cup sour cream

To make the caviar, place the lentils in a small pot and add the water, salt, kombu, and garlic. Bring the liquid just to a boil, then reduce the heat so that the liquid is simmering. Cook until the lentils are tender but hold their shape, 15 to 20 minutes. Remove from the heat and let the lentils cool in the liquid. Drain and discard the kombu and garlic. Place the lentils in a bowl and gently stir in the capers, brine, and olive oil, if desired. Set aside, covered with a kitchen towel.

To make the blini, in a saucepan, warm the milk until it reads 100°F on an instant-read thermometer. Add the yeast and set aside. In a bowl, combine the flour, sugar, and salt. In another bowl, whisk the egg yolks and slowly drizzle in the oil to emulsify. Pour about one-fourth of the flour mixture through a fine-mesh sieve over the egg mixture. Then, whisk in one-fourth of the milk-yeast mixture until smooth. Continue to add the ingredients and whisk until all of the mixtures are incorporated. Cover and let stand for 1 hour.

When you're ready to cook, whip the egg whites to soft peaks. Gently fold the egg whites into the batter. Finally, fold in chives. Transfer the batter to a plastic squeeze bottle.

Heat a sauté pan over medium heat with 1 tablespoon oil. Working in batches, pipe 1 tablespoon of blini batter into the pan, and repeat to fill up the pan, leaving about 2 inches of space between each one. As soon as the blini start to bubble, after about 30 seconds, flip to cook the other side. When the second side is golden brown, transfer to a paper towel-lined plate to cool slightly.

To serve, smear each blini with a dollop of sour cream, then a spoonful of the lentils, and finish with a sprinkle of chives.

SMOKED SALMON CAVIAR

This recipe title might seem confusing. It's not roe from smoked salmon; rather, it's salmon roe that we smoke after we cure it. We cooked a dinner at the prestigious James Beard House in New York City, and we served these little jewels on one of our dishes. Try them on a cracker or as a garnish for a main course dish, or even lightly tossed into pasta for a little pop of flavor.

MAKES 2 CUPS SMOKED SALMON CAVIAR

½ cup sea salt	1 tablespoon soy sauce
3 cups water	Juice of ½ lemon
2 cups fresh salmon eggs	3 tablespoons alder wood chips

In a small bowl, dissolve the salt in the water. Break the roe sac of the salmon eggs and empty the eggs into a large bowl. Remove as much of the membrane as possible. (We have a roasting rack with a mesh large enough for eggs to drop through, leaving the membrane behind.) Gently pour the saltwater mixture (brine), the soy sauce, and lemon juice over the eggs and let stand for at least 1 hour or up to 4 hours.

Drain the eggs through a fine-mesh strainer and rinse gently in cold water. Remove any white particles that might remain from the egg sac casings.

In a 6-quart casserole with a tight-fitting lid, fit a piece of aluminum foil into the bottom of the pot. Place the wood chips over the foil. Place an additional piece of foil over the wood chips. Turn on your kitchen ventilation. Heat the pot on the stove top over medium heat until the wood chips are smoking, about 5 minutes. Place a steamer or rack that fits into the pot on top of the foil. Place a heatproof plate or bowl on top of the steamer or rack, add the rinsed salmon eggs, and cover the pot. Turn the heat off. Let the salmon eggs absorb the smoke in the covered pot for about 30 minutes.

Store the caviar in the refrigerator in a clean glass jar. The caviar will keep for up to 2 weeks.

BAKED BEANS & GREENS

Kirsten's husband, Carl, loves baked beans. He is a picky eater, but not when it comes to these beans. You don't have to add greens and vegetables as we do if you want a more traditional baked bean dish. Also, you could add cooked bacon or ground beef. We like to keep our version meat-free.

MAKES 6 SERVINGS

1 pound dried pinto beans

1 bay leaf

1 sprig fresh thyme

6 cups store-bought or homemade chicken or vegetable stock

2 tablespoons canola oil

1 large yellow onion, diced

3 garlic cloves, minced

1 bunch Swiss chard, stems removed and diced, leaves torn into bite-size pieces

1 cup mixed mushrooms, torn into bite-size pieces

2 stalks celery, finely diced

2 carrots, peeled and finely diced

4 large tomatoes, diced

1 cup ketchup

½ cup packed dark brown sugar

¼ cup molasses

¼ cup birch (or other) syrup

¼ cup Worcestershire sauce

¼ cup apple cider vinegar

1 teaspoon sea salt

½ teaspoon coarsely ground black pepper

Place the beans in a 6-quart casserole and add enough water to cover them by 2 inches. Add the bay leaf and thyme sprig. Bring the liquid to a boil over high heat; boil the beans for 2 minutes, then remove from the heat and let stand for 1 hour.

Drain and rinse beans, discarding the liquid, bay leaf, and thyme. Return the beans to the pot and add the stock. Bring to a boil over high heat, then immediately reduce the heat so that the liquid just simmers. Simmer until beans are almost tender, about 1 hour.

While the beans are cooking, in another 6-quart casserole over medium heat, warm the oil. Add the onion and sauté until tender, 5 to 7 minutes. Add the garlic, Swiss chard, mushrooms, celery, carrots, and tomatoes. Sauté until the

carrots are tender, about 5 minutes. Stir in the ketchup, brown sugar, molasses, birch syrup, Worcestershire sauce, vinegar, salt, and pepper. Remove from the heat.

Preheat the oven to 300°F.

Drain the beans, reserving the cooking liquid. Place the beans into the casserole containing the vegetable mixture and stir to combine. Cover with the lid and bake until the beans are tender and the sauce has thickened, about 2 hours, stirring every 30 minutes. Add the reserved cooking liquid as needed to loosen the beans if they get a little bit dry.

Serve warm.

SPRUCE TIP BUTTERMILK CAKE

We've learned to love the flavor of early spring spruce tips, the bright green new buds that surround us everywhere. We pick them when they are young and tender and preserve them for other times of the year. We make spruce tips into powders and oils, put them in cookies and savory dishes, and, as you see here, in cakes in the form of spruce sugar. Spruce tips are available for sale online.

MAKES 12 TO 20 SERVINGS

FOR THE CAKE

¾ cup unsalted butter, at room temperature, plus more for greasing

3 cups cake flour, sifted

2 teaspoons baking powder

½ teaspoon baking soda

½ teaspoon sea salt

1¼ cups buttermilk

¼ cup canola oil

1 tablespoon pure vanilla bean paste or vanilla extract

1½ cups granulated sugar

½ cup Spruce Sugar (page 293)

4 large eggs

FOR THE FROSTING

½ cup unsalted butter, at room temperature

8 ounces cream cheese, at room temperature

1 teaspoon pure vanilla bean paste or vanilla extract

½ teaspoon sea salt

2 cups Spruce Sugar (page 293)

To make the cake, preheat the oven to 350°F. Line a 9-by-13-inch cake pan with parchment paper and grease well with butter.

In a bowl, sift together the flour, baking powder, baking soda, and salt. Set aside. In another bowl, mix together the buttermilk, oil, and vanilla. Set aside.

In a mixer fitted with the whisk attachment, beat the ¾ cup butter, granulated sugar, and spruce sugar on medium speed until lightened in color and fluffy, about 2 minutes. Add the eggs one at a time, mixing until incorporated. Scrape down the sides of the bowl. Add the flour mixture in 1 cup additions alternately with the buttermilk mixture in ½-cup additions, beating on low speed until just incorporated; be careful not to overmix. Scrape the batter into the prepared pan, smoothing out with a rubber spatula, and place into the oven. Bake until the cake is lightly golden and firm to the touch, and a cake tester comes out clean, about 25 minutes.

Remove the cake from the oven and let cool in the pan for 10 minutes. Invert the cake out onto a platter. Cool the cake completely.

To make the frosting, in the bowl of a stand mixer fitted with the whisk attachment, beat the butter and cream cheese on low speed until creamy and lump-free, about 5 minutes. Add the vanilla and salt and mix well. With the mixer running, slowly pour in the Spruce Sugar and mix on medium until creamy.

Frost the cooled cake and then cut it into squares to serve.

RED CURRANT TART

Red currants are everywhere at Winterlake Lodge, while salmonberries proliferate at Tutka Bay. As such, in the summertime we never lack for delicious berry options to make into pies or tarts. This tart is a beauty and it is always consumed quickly. If you don't have an open bottle of sparkling wine handy, water works fine, too. This tart is delicious on its own but also goes great with Chocolate Semifreddo (page 242).

MAKES 6 TO 8 SERVINGS

1 cup fresh red currants

1 cup sparkling wine

1 cup sugar

1 cinnamon stick

1 tablespoon spruce tips

½ teaspoon sea salt

½ cup unsalted butter, at room temperature

2 eggs plus 2 egg yolks

½ teaspoon pure vanilla bean paste or vanilla extract

1 pre-baked Tart Shell (page 294)

Preheat the oven to 325°F.

In a heavy-bottomed saucepan over medium heat, combine the currants, sparkling wine, sugar, cinnamon stick, spruce tips, and salt. Bring just to a boil over high heat and then reduce the heat to medium-low and simmer for 10 minutes. Using a rubber spatula, press the hot mixture through a fine-mesh sieve into a bowl. Add the butter and slowly stir. Let cool slightly.

In a clean bowl, beat the eggs and egg yolks with the vanilla paste until blended. While whisking, carefully pour in the red currant mixture while whisking (if the currant mixture is too hot, it will cook the egg). Pour the mixture into a clean saucepan. Cook over medium heat, stirring constantly just until barely boiling. Pour the hot mixture into the tart shell.

Bake the tart until the curd is set and firm to the touch, about 15 minutes. Cool completely.

Cut the cooled tart into wedges to serve.

THE HEALING GARDEN

We have two kinds of gardens in our lives—cultivated and wild. Each is as beloved and as important as the other. Our cultivated gardens are attempts at growing what we can within our intense summer schedules. We're blessed with long northern summer sun, fertile, loamy soil, and plenty of eager hands to help with garden chores. Even the kids jump in. But there are downsides to gardening in the wild: porcupines, moose, bears, beavers, and sled dogs (at Winterlake). There was once a wild goat at Tutka Bay Lodge that decided to camp in the garden for a good two weeks. Mandy and Neil were caretaking and buttoning the lodge down to prepare for winter when they were startled to find the goat firmly planted in the garden near the lodge front door. His rippling muscles were almost comical, but they worked to intimidate 6-foot-2-inch Neil.

Mandy and Neil were held captive in the lodge for a day and a night before they felt the goat had wandered as far as the big deck, and they could go about their outside chores. Perhaps an average Alaska family might have just shot the goat and trimmed him up for the winter freezer, but Kirsten asked Mandy and Neil specifically if they would not hurt the wild garden goat. He might be magic. So, now we have an idea in our family that goats have magical powers. The next summer, our garden was quite lovely, and the Nootka roses along the garden edge bloomed vigorously (and, the year before, they didn't bloom at all). Proof of the goat's magic?

We have quite a bit of magical thinking in our lives. How could we not when we see so much magic in the natural world around us every day? We perhaps in our hearts know our bits of household magic ritual (throwing notes on bits of paper into a fire to rid us of negatives, serving crab on New Year's Eve for good luck, or washing rice three times) doesn't alter any universal outcomes, but we do them all the same.

The best magic we see is in the early spring when it seems that nothing living could come from the feet of deep snow on the ground. The first to push up through it all, pressing toward the sun, is the rhubarb we have planted at Tutka Bay. These are the same rhubarb plants we first planted nearly forty years ago at Riversong Lodge, where we had our first garden. A Riversong employee who stayed long after we sold the lodge and moved away sent us the rhubarb roots as a gift—the best gift ever!

We have quite a bit of magical thinking in our lives.

Rhubarb unfurls from the snow with a vibrant green curl that is a shocking portent to what the garden will soon be. Each day, we stop by and see another inch, another furl of a new leaf, and soon, bright buds burst to become red stalks that shoot straight toward the sun. The leaves grow so large, we sometimes wear them as sunhats in the garden. Rhubarb comes from Mongolia, a country just about the same size as Alaska but with millions more people. The stalks were once four times more valuable than opium in England. And, here it is in our garden. That is pure magic.

Our favorite use for rhubarb, still, after forty years, is our rhubarb chutney. We've included a recipe for our chutney in the pantry section (see page 291) because we've highlighted it so many times in all our previous books, but we just couldn't bear leave it out. It's too close to our hearts. The color of a bright green inner rhubarb stalk, the deep red outside stalk, and the deep green leaves are forever a favorite summer color palette.

The first things to arrive in the wild at Winterlake Lodge are tiny blue and purple woodland violets, usually near the small alder trees along the trail that leads to Red Lake, about a mile behind the lodge. These early arrivals are fresh and brilliant accompaniments against a first-caught King salmon. If we are lucky and we can pick three cups of wild violets, we can make a jar of jelly (see page 283). There is nothing quite as lovely as a jar of wild violet jelly sitting on the pantry shelf.

> The range and breadth of our wild gathering is diverse and formidable.

The garden at Tutka Bay Lodge isn't so big in footprint as the one at Winterlake, but it has captivated many a heart. It winds along a lovely path to our massage cabin and then on to the greenhouse. To the left of the cabin, there is a pathway leading to a teak bench seating area that offers a contemplative and restful place to sit and admire the peacefulness of the garden. Carl commissioned the design of this small but elegant space in 2013 when Kirsten was diagnosed with breast cancer. No one in our family had ever been seriously ill before, and it was a scare and a shock for us all. The garden project was a way for Carl to express his grief and concern for Kirsten when he found words to be too difficult. He's always been a show-don't-tell kind of person when it comes to communicating difficult emotions.

In our Tutka Bay garden, we have several lilac trees, two cherry trees in the greenhouse, and showy Alaska garden favorites such as delphinium and columbine. Gus, our boat captain, hauled buckets of shells and rocks up from the beach to line the pathway. We have a small older greenhouse that we use to grow beds of microgreens. We love that the beds are at hand-height, so we don't have to bend down to pick them. Chefs can walk to the garden and snip tops of tiny pea shoots or radish sprouts to garnish their dishes and make even simple soups or salads look elegant.

The foraging season at Tutka Bay Lodge starts early and lasts until the first hard frost. We gather sea edibles such as beach greens and sea lettuce at the same time we gather forest edibles like hedgehog mushrooms and spruce tips. The range and breadth of our wild gathering is diverse and formidable. We also look for lovely wildflowers that grace our tables in vases or on plates. Kirsten's favorite is a delicate white flower that hangs its little bell toward the ground. We call these "frog's reading lamps." We are sure there is a more official name for these out there.

At Winterlake Lodge, at least a thousand feet higher in elevation than Tutka Bay, we find blueberries as far as the eye can see. From the helicopters we use to access much of the Alaska Range, we see bears grazing over vast fields of these alpine berries. There are also currants and cranberries, and a delicate little treasure called a "nagoonberry," which is a sumptuous cross between a raspberry and a strawberry (this is our own taste interpretation). Red currants hang like dangling jewels in the undergrowth, and a hundred types of mushrooms hide in the tree wells all along the Iditarod Trail.

Gathered and grown, along the ocean or in the mountains, our intimate gardens and the bigger gardens of our local wild landscapes bring a sense of adventure and wonderment to our tables.

CHOCOLATE MINT OLIVE OIL CAKE

This olive oil cake is a favorite and we like to serve it with fresh berries and mint branches scattered on the serving platter. Nothing is lovelier than to sit in our garden and watch hundreds of birds dart and dash through rose bushes and watch the spectacle of the summer beauty.

MAKES 12 SERVINGS

Canola oil for greasing

1 cup plus 3 tablespoons unsweetened cocoa powder

½ cup fresh mint leaves, cut into fine strips (chiffonade)

1½ cups boiling water

½ teaspoon pure vanilla bean paste or vanilla extract

1 tablespoon distilled white vinegar

¾ cup plus 4 tablespoons fruity olive oil

1½ cups all-purpose flour

2 teaspoons baking soda

1 teaspoon sea salt

1 cup granulated sugar

¾ cup packed light brown sugar

1 cup semisweet chocolate chips

¼ cup roughly chopped fresh mint

1 tablespoon honey

Preheat the oven to 325°F. Line the bottom of a 9-inch round cake pan with parchment paper and grease the bottom and sides with oil.

In a heatproof bowl, whisk together 1 cup of the cocoa powder, the mint, and boiling water until it makes a smooth paste. Whisk in the vanilla, vinegar, and ¾ cup olive oil. In a separate bowl, stir together the flour, baking soda, and salt. Add the granulated and brown sugars to the cocoa powder-mint mixture, whisking until combined. Then, add the flour mixture to the cocoa powder-mint mixture, folding the mixtures together well.

Pour the batter into the prepared pan. Bake until the cake feels firm to the touch, about 30 minutes. Cool the cake in the pan on a wire rack for 10 minutes. Then, gently flip the cake out onto a cooling rack, peel off the parchment, and let the cake cool completely.

In a heatproof bowl set over (not touching) a pan of simmering water, combine the chocolate chips, roughly chopped mint, remaining 3 tablespoons cocoa powder, remaining 4 tablespoons olive oil, and the honey. Keep over the heat until the chocolate melts completely, then remove from the heat and whisk until smooth. Strain the mixture through a fine mesh sieve into a small bowl.

Pour the melted chocolate mixture over the cooled cake and use a spatula to spread it evenly. Let the cake stand for 5 minutes. Cut into wedges and serve.

ELI'S SMOKY OLD FASHIONED

Eli is one of our long-time wilderness guides and naturalists. He crafted this drink in the springtime after he tapped surrounding birch trees for sap and made syrup. Eli is quite the entertainer at appetizer hour. He begins the process of making this cocktail using a glass smoked with alder, the same wood we use to smoke salmon. He replaces the traditional sugar cube with locally harvested birch syrup.

MAKES 1 SERVING

Small piece of alder wood
1 orange wedge
1 teaspoon (5 ml) birch syrup

2 dashes aromatic bitters
2 ounces (60 ml) bourbon whiskey

Using a small handheld kitchen torch, heat the alder wood to produce smoke and place it on a flameproof surface. Place a cocktail glass upside down over the smoldering wood to capture the aroma.

Carefully peel the flesh from the peel of the orange wedge and place the flesh in a cocktail shaker. Add the birch syrup and bitters to the shaker and muddle until the orange flesh is sufficiently pressed. Add the bourbon to the shaker and stir. Remove the glass from the alder wood and add the contents of the shaker to the glass. Add 3 to 4 ice cubes and swirl lightly. Twist the orange peel and place it in the glass for garnish.

Serve immediately.

ZUCCHINI CAKES WITH MISO GLAZE

Mandy loves miso on or in everything, such as these loaf cakes made from the zucchini in our garden. These loaves are just as good with a bit of chocolate chunks added in as well. We just brush a light amount of glaze over the top of the loaves, but you can pile it on as thickly as you like.

MAKES ABOUT 12 SERVINGS

FOR THE ZUCCHINI CAKES
3½ cups all-purpose flour
1 cup whole-wheat flour
1½ teaspoons baking powder
1½ teaspoons baking soda
1 teaspoon sea salt
¼ teaspoon ground cinnamon
4 large eggs
1½ cups granulated sugar

1½ cups packed light brown sugar
1½ cups canola oil
3 zucchini, shredded

FOR THE MISO GLAZE
2 tablespoons unsalted butter
1 tablespoon mild white (shiro) miso
2 cups powdered sugar
1 teaspoon pure vanilla paste
   or vanilla extract

Preheat the oven to 325°F. Grease two 8½-by-4½-by-2¾-inch loaf pans.

In a bowl, mix together both flours, the baking powder, baking soda, salt, and cinnamon. In a large bowl, whisk together the eggs, both sugars, and oil until blended. Add the zucchini and flour mixture and mix with a whisk until just blended. Pour the batter into the prepared loaf pans, filling them halfway. Bake the cakes until a cake tester comes out clean when inserted into the center, 25 to 30 minutes.

Cool the cakes in the pans for about 10 minutes, then remove from the pans and place on a platter.

To make the glaze, place the butter and miso into a small sauté pan over low heat and melt the butter. Stir to dissolve the miso. Remove from the heat and add the sugar and vanilla and mix well.

Spread the glaze over the tops of the cakes. Let the cakes stand for 15 minutes to set the glaze before serving.

Cut into slices to serve.

GARDEN MINT CHOCOLATE SANDWICH COOKIES

We have so much mint in our gardens. The herb survives brutal winters, hot summers, and anything else that Mother Nature throws at it. We love to point out the square stems to guests in the garden. Our favorite garden mint varieties are chocolate mint, orange mint, and straight-up peppermint.

MAKES 48 COOKIES

FOR THE GANACHE
1 cup heavy cream
2 tablespoons unsalted butter
1 cup fresh mint leaves
2 cups semisweet chocolate chips
Pinch of sea salt

FOR THE COOKIES
1½ cups unsalted butter, at room temperature
1½ cups powdered sugar, sifted
3½ cups cake flour, sifted, plus more for dusting
1 cup unsweetened cocoa powder
Small whole mint leaves for garnish (optional)

To make the ganache, in a small saucepan, combine the heavy cream, butter, and mint. Warm over low heat until the butter has melted and the cream is warm. Remove from the heat and let steep for 5 minutes. Pour the mixture through a fine-mesh strainer into a bowl, discarding the mint. Add the chocolate chips to a bowl and pour over the hot cream mixture. Allow the mixture to stand for about 5 minutes to soften the chocolate chips completely. Stir until smooth. Cover and let stand at room temperature for 2 hours or up to overnight.

To make the cookies, in the bowl of a stand mixer fitted with the paddle attachment, cream the butter and sugar until light and fluffy, about 2 minutes. On low speed, mix in the flour and cocoa powder well. Divide the dough in half. Place each half on a lightly floured work surface and shape it into a roll about 12 inches long. Wrap each

roll in a clean kitchen towel and chill for 20 minutes. Meanwhile, preheat the oven to 350°F.

Remove the dough logs from the refrigerator and cut each log into ¼-inch slices. Place the slices onto 4 nonstick baking sheets (or use 2 baking sheets in batches), 24 cookies on each pan, spacing them 1 inch apart, and bake until the tops are no longer moist, about 10 minutes. Transfer to wire racks and let cool completely.

To assemble, spread about 1 tablespoon of the ganache onto half of the cookies. Place the other half of the cookies on top of the ganache, lining up the cookie edges, to make sandwiches. For a pretty look, you can press small mint leaves around the sides of the cookies helping them to adhere to the protruding ganache.

SMOKED SALMON CAULIFLOWER BISCUITS

This is a wheat-free recipe, which we get quite a few requests for these days. Cauliflower grows well in our garden and we are learning how to use it creatively. We add in smoked salmon and cheddar cheese, which, surprisingly, are good flavor matches.

MAKES 8 BISCUITS

Water, as needed

Sea salt

1 pound cauliflower florets

2 large cloves garlic, thinly sliced

1 cup plus 2 tablespoons grated white cheddar cheese

2 large eggs

3 tablespoons minced fresh chives

½ cup flaked hot-smoked (kippered) salmon

1 tablespoon cornstarch

Preheat the oven to 375°F. Line a baking sheet with parchment paper.

Fill a large saucepan with water and add 1 teaspoon of salt. Bring the water to a boil over high heat. When the water boils, reduce the heat so that the water is at a rolling simmer and add the cauliflower and garlic. Simmer until the cauliflower is soft, about 10 minutes, then remove the cauliflower and garlic from the water with a slotted spoon. Transfer the cauliflower and garlic to a piece of damp cheesecloth and wring out the excess moisture. Transfer the cauliflower and garlic to a food processor and puree until smooth.

Place the cauliflower mixture into a bowl and add 1 cup of the cheese, the eggs, chives, salmon, cornstarch, and salt to taste. Stir until thoroughly mixed. Using about ⅓ cup (well packed) of the cauliflower mixture for each biscuit, scoop the mixture onto the parchment paper, leaving about 1 inch between each one, to make 8 biscuits. Sprinkle the tops with the remaining 2 tablespoons cheese. Bake until the biscuits are browned and crispy around the edges, about 30 minutes.

Serve warm.

SAVORY DRIED TOMATO-SESAME COOKIES

Sometimes you just don't feel like a sweet cookie, but something savory and crunchy instead. This cookie fits the bill and we keep them at our lodge coffee bar alongside the usual sweet suspects. We've been making variations of this same cookie for many years and we haven't found anyone yet who doesn't like them.

MAKES 12 COOKIES

1 cup shredded cheddar cheese

1 cup unsalted butter, at room temperature

1 large egg

1 cup all-purpose flour, plus extra for dusting

½ teaspoon baking powder

1 teaspoon piment d'esplette or pure chile powder

Sea salt and freshly ground black pepper

½ cup oil-packed sun-dried tomatoes, drained, patted dry, and diced

1 tablespoon minced fresh basil

½ cup sesame seeds, toasted

In a bowl, combine the cheese, butter, and egg and mix until smooth. Stir in the flour, baking powder, piment d'esplette, and ½ teaspoon of salt and ½ teaspoon pepper. Stir in the tomatoes, basil, and sesame seeds. Cover the dough with a kitchen towel and chill thoroughly in the refrigerator for about 30 minutes.

Preheat the oven to 350°F. Line a 13-by-18-inch rimmed baking sheet with parchment paper.

Remove the dough from the refrigerator and roll it out on a lightly floured surface until ¼-inch thick. Cut out the cookies with a 3-inch round cutter or a downturned drinking glass. Transfer the cookies to the prepared baking sheet, spacing them 1 inch apart.

Bake the cookies until light golden brown, about 10 minutes. Remove from the oven and let cool completely, allowing them to firm up before serving.

BROCCOLI LEAF PASTA

We have a "leave no edible behind" motto and love to use the entire plants of our vegetables whenever we can. Broccoli leaves are delicious used just as they are tossed into salads and pastas, or as a blended sauce as in this recipe. Just pick off the small leaves that grow along a broccoli stalk. Save any stems from the broccoli leaves and reserve them for something else. For example, you can dice them and cook them like broccoli in a stir-fry or soup.

MAKES 4 SERVINGS

Sea salt and freshly ground black pepper

1 pound broccoli leaves

6 cloves garlic, sliced

1 shallot, sliced

1 bunch flat-leaf parsley, chopped

5 tablespoons extra-virgin olive oil

½ cup grated Parmigiano-Reggiano cheese

8 ounces dried spaghetti

1 tablespoon unsalted butter

1 cup ricotta cheese

1 tablespoon finely grated lemon zest

Bring a saucepan of salted water to a rolling boil over medium-high heat. Tear the broccoli leaves into pieces. Add the leaves, garlic, and shallot to the salted water and cook for 1 minute (this is called blanching).

Use tongs to transfer the broccoli leaves to a blender; then, dip a hand-held strainer into the blanching water to retrieve the shallot and garlic and add these to the blender as well. Add the parsley to the blender. Leave the water in the pot and bring it back to a boil (for cooking the spaghetti). Remove a ¼ cup of the blanching water and add that to the blender. Run the blender on low for a few minutes to begin to chop the ingredients. Then, turn the speed to high until the mixture is very smooth, about 1 minute. Pour the olive oil into the blender, and then the Parmigiano-Reggiano. Blend on high to incorporate the oil and the cheese. The sauce should be smooth. Taste and season with salt and pepper.

Cook the pasta in the boiling water until al dente. When the pasta is done, reserve 1 cup of the cooking water before draining. Return the pasta to the pot and add the butter. Add the green broccoli sauce and toss the pasta to coat it well with the sauce. Loosen the sauce with a bit of pasta water if needed.

Divide the pasta among serving bowls and top each bowl with dollops of the ricotta and a sprinkle of lemon zest.

WILDFLOWER-BARLEY TISANE

We make plenty of iterations of wild tisanes (medicinal drinks or infusions, similar to tea, but made without tea leaves). This tea has a Japanese influence with the barley added. It is a lovely drink and it makes us feel like we are sipping on something that's very healthful.

MAKES 8 CUPS

½ cup pearled barley

8 cups water

½ cup dried edible wildflowers,
    such as rose petals, fireweed,
    marigolds, or dandelions

2 tablespoons honey

1 teaspoon pure vanilla bean paste
    or vanilla extract

Place the barley in a dry, nonstick sauté pan over low heat and toast, stirring constantly, until it is a deep golden brown, about 5 minutes.

In a large saucepan over high heat, bring the water to a boil. Add the toasted barley and wildflowers and immediately reduce the heat so that the water is at a low simmer; simmer until the mixture is aromatic, about 5 minutes.

Remove the pot from the heat and use a hand-held strainer to remove the barley and flower petals from the pot. Stir in the honey and vanilla. Serve hot, or cool completely and serve iced.

RHUBARB KIMCHI

Kimchi is a beautiful addition to a simple dish of rice and salmon. This version doesn't use the better-known Napa cabbage, but our own garden rhubarb, which we always have in abundance. Raspberry concentrate is sold in health food stores and through online sources and adds a lovely color. Look for dried shrimp in any Asian market.

MAKES 5 CUPS

4 cups peeled and thinly sliced rhubarb

½ cup raspberry juice concentrate

1 cup thinly sliced green onions

2 tablespoons sweet white rice flour

2 cups water

2 tablespoons packed light brown sugar

3 cloves garlic, thinly sliced

½ yellow onion, finely diced

¼-inch knob ginger, peeled and diced

¼ cup small dried shrimp

¼ cup Korean red pepper flakes (or to taste)

1 tablespoon fish sauce (Nam Pla)

Place the rhubarb, raspberry juice, and green onions in a large bowl. Set aside.

In a small saucepan, combine the rice flour and water. Place the pan over medium heat and bring the liquid to a boil. Add the brown sugar and simmer until the mixture starts to thicken, about 2 minutes. Remove from the heat.

In a food processor combine the garlic, yellow onion, and ginger. Blend until a rough paste forms. Add the shrimp, pepper flakes, and fish sauce and pulse the blender 2 to 3 times to blend.

Pour the rice flour mixture into a bowl. Add the onion-shrimp mixture and whisk together until blended; this is the kimchi base. Pour the kimchi base into the bowl with the rhubarb mixture and stir well.

Transfer the kimchi mixture to clean glass canning jars, topping each with a piece of cheesecloth, and securing with a rubber band. Place the jars onto a baking sheet to catch any overflow. Allow the kimchi to stand at room temperature for 24 hours to begin the fermentation process.

After 24 hours, remove the cheesecloth and rubber bands. Place lids loosely on the canning jars and place them in the refrigerator. The kimchi will continue to ferment so you will need to release the gas in the jar daily by lifting each lid briefly. Kimchi can be eaten fresh but will be best after about 1 week of fermentation.

CARROT SALAD WITH SORREL DRESSING

This looks like a time-consuming recipe, but it's not. We have grown sorrel in our garden ever since we've had a garden. It adds a refreshing sour lemon note to the dressing here. We like barley couscous, but big Israeli couscous or other wheat-based grains are great in this salad as well. We serve this alongside fresh grilled fish and sliced tomatoes.

MAKES 6 SERVINGS

FOR THE SORREL DRESSING

2 cups cleaned sorrel leaves

1 clove garlic, chopped

½ cup plain yogurt

½ cup mayonnaise

1 teaspoon Dijon mustard

1 tablespoon finely minced fresh chives

1 tablespoon apple cider vinegar

Sea salt and freshly ground black pepper

FOR THE SALAD

1 tablespoon pure chile powder

1 tablespoon ground cumin

1 tablespoon granulated garlic

1 teaspoon ground turmeric

¼ teaspoon cayenne pepper

Sea salt and freshly ground black pepper

¼ cup honey

2 (15-ounce) cans chickpeas

½ cup extra-virgin olive oil

1 pound large orange carrots, peeled and cut on the bias into ½-inch pieces

1 pound red carrots, peeled, and cut lengthwise into quarters

2½ cups barley couscous

½ cup sliced almonds, toasted

1 small bunch fresh flat-leaf parsley, chopped

½ cup dried currants

2 cups arugula

To make the dressing, roughly chop the sorrel and add to a food processor. Add the garlic and yogurt. Process until a smooth puree forms. Transfer to a small bowl and stir in the mayonnaise, mustard, chives, and vinegar. Season to taste with salt and pepper. Cover and refrigerate until needed.

Preheat the oven to 400°F. Line 2 rimmed baking sheets with parchment paper.

To make the salad, in a small bowl, mix together the chile powder, cumin, granulated garlic, turmeric, cayenne pepper, 1 teaspoon salt, and the honey.

Drain and rinse the chickpeas and place them in another bowl. Drizzle with a few tablespoons of the olive oil and 1 tablespoon of the spice mixture. Pour the chickpeas onto a prepared baking sheet. Bake the chickpeas until crisp, about 15 minutes.

Place the carrots in a bowl and toss with remaining olive oil and spice mixture. Season lightly with salt and pepper. Arrange the carrots in a single layer on the second baking sheet. Roast until tender, 15 to 20 minutes.

Cook the couscous according to the package instructions. When done, fluff the couscous grains with a fork and stir in the almonds, parsley, and currants.

Divide the couscous mixture among serving bowls and top with the roasted carrots, crisped chickpeas, and arugula. Pass the dressing at the table for drizzling.

ZERO-WASTE VEGETABLE CRISPS

This recipe works great for random kale leaves or hearty greens as well as peels from carrots, potatoes, and any vegetables or hard fruits you peel. Save the peels in the refrigerator or freezer until you gather enough to make a batch. These savory, crunchy chips just might be a new movie-night tradition. Use any leftover seasoning for additional batches or grilled vegetables and fish.

MAKES 2 CUPS

1 teaspoon cornstarch

2 teaspoons ground nutmeg

2 teaspoons ground coriander

2 teaspoons ground cumin

2 teaspoons ground ginger

2 teaspoons turmeric

2 teaspoons sea salt

2 teaspoons ground cinnamon

1½ teaspoons sugar

1½ teaspoons paprika

1½ teaspoons freshly ground black pepper

1 teaspoon cayenne pepper

1 teaspoon ground cardamom

1 tablespoon Granulated Garlic (page 290)

2 cups mixed vegetable or fruit peelings, such as potato, carrot, parsnip, apple, sweet potato, beet

3 tablespoons extra-virgin olive oil

Preheat the oven to 400°F. Line a standard rimmed baking sheet with parchment paper.

In a bowl, combine the cornstarch, nutmeg, coriander, cumin, ginger, turmeric, salt, cinnamon, sugar, paprika, black pepper, cayenne, cardamom, and garlic.

Spread out the vegetable peelings evenly onto the parchment. Drizzle the oil over all of the peelings, toss well with the oil, and spread out again. Place in the oven and bake until golden and crispy, 15 to 20 minutes.

Remove the crisps from the oven and place them into a bowl. Sprinkle the seasoning mix onto the crisps to taste (there will be some seasoning mix left over). Store the additional seasoning in a jar with a lid for up to 1 month.

Serve right away.

A MILLION-ACRE PICNIC

If you travel north from Anchorage and then turn west, you'll eventually approach the Alaska Range, the location of Winterlake Lodge. And there you'll find a Robinson R-44 helicopter waiting to take you to some of the most remarkable terrains on the planet.

Every morning during the summer, a red-painted helicopter lifts from the helipad located in front of the old Trapper's Cabin along the east end of the lake. The helicopter rotors wash over an old, forgotten garden where a few ancient rhubarb plants peek out from the cow parsnip and ferns. They all bend against the whirlwind created as the helicopter lifts and turns above the lake and beyond to the north. The Trapper Cabin stands sturdy and silent, almost defiant against our modernization. The cabin, built long ago, isn't used for guests anymore, but it is an intact museum of sorts from the days when a trapper named Gene Leonard lived there.

In those days, life was very different at Winterlake Lodge. It was the early 1950s and the lodge had already been around for twenty years. It was called Hayes River Lodge and used as a hunting camp. Owner Gene Leonard made his living by trapping animals and selling their fur to a buyer in Anchorage. There are still remnants of Gene's trapline in the woods near the lodge. We can see old tin cans nailed onto trees. These cans were once filled with food to lure animals to the deadly snares hidden in the brush. It seems like such a ghastly business, but for Gene Leonard, it was how he made a living.

As we lift into the air, we can see the marks of Gene's old trapline weaving through the woods behind the lodge, and we can see Red Lake, a smaller lake situated about a mile behind us, occupied by several pairs of nesting swans. And then we see the mountains rising in the west, with jagged peaks and vast snowy summits that seem to go on forever. The helicopter flies low over first the Skwentna River and then the Hayes River, a 23-mile river that starts from the Hayes Glacier and flows back into the Skwentna. Old glaciers running into old rivers braid across the landscape, with water so cold and fast, it cuts right through rock to create deep and scenic canyons, always heading toward and eventually making its way to the sea. As the helicopter flies higher in elevation, fantastical shapes of solid ice rise up around us. Cathedrals, pillars, domes, and caves make us feel like we are in someplace ancient and holy—and we are. Deep blue pools of glacial water punctuate the ice floor. Sometimes we land the helicopter and dive right in.

This is our own backyard wonderland.

We've served food in the most adventurous of places: on a glacier, in a raft, on a riverside over a campfire, on Denali Mountain, delivered by dog team, on a yacht, on a cruise ship, in a cave—we could go on. But one lovely ritual we do over again is to take guests up to the top of the Wolverine Ridge behind us. The ridge, about four thousand feet in elevation, is where we can look over our entire broad valley and toward the Kichatna Spires, a section of the 400-mile Alaska Range. This is our own backyard wonderland. The Spires are jagged granite rock peaks that form a craggy, citadel-like ridgeline worthy of any Middle Earth quest. It's a place for braver folks than us to conquer. But when we sit on top of Wolverine Ridge and look toward it, our imaginations are filled with dreams of this faraway and largely inaccessible place.

Wolverine Ridge, far above the tree line, is a vast space to sit and look out over the world. Tiny purple, scarlet, and white alpine flowers cover the ground in a thick mat, and there are bear dens dotted along the hillside. Peregrine falcons fly overhead, and sometimes we even see a wayward eagle or two. We spread out our picnic blankets and display our feast over the best lunch spot in the world. Down below, the lodge, the dog lot, the garden, the dock on the lake, and the trails all look like the panorama of a small toy town.

We Alaskans, bears and humans, know how to eat well within the wild.

A favorite outdoor luncheon dish is Moroccan flatbread we've renamed "wild bread." We've been to Morocco many times. One year, we met a young man who cooked for us in a small, colorfully eclectic restaurant called La Fromagerie outside of the port city of Essaouira. Hicham Hnini taught us how to make camel cheese. He served us a lovely dinner in an open-air space filled with antiques and artifacts from the restaurant's French owner. Two years later, we brought Hicham to Alaska, and he lived with us for a year. He taught at our cooking school, working in the Tutka Bay Lodge kitchen and sharing his creative and exotic Moroccan dishes with us. While we are writing this book, Hicham is back in Morocco cooking, but he promises us he will return.

In our efforts to eliminate single-use plastics, we have been relying upon alternatives for packaging foods for the field. Bee's Wrap is a favorite. We use plenty of butcher-shop brown paper and thin brown twine to package up snacks for guests. They always look lovely and a bit old-fashioned, but sometimes in the snow or weather, they don't hold up as well as we would like. We use aluminum foil reluctantly—better than plastic, we suppose. And, silicone pouches help. These are complicated times to understand and know what is truly eco-friendly. We all do the best we can.

When Carl takes guests rafting on Happy River, we love to set up a campsite around a bend out of view from the rafters. The exhilarated but hungry rafters come around the corner and discover us. It's the best kind of surprise; there, they find heat from a roaring fire, hot food bubbling over the wood, a camp table set up with salads, sandwiches, and cookies. We always try to pack light in consideration of having to helicopter in our supplies, but we don't skimp on little essentials, such as cloth napkins or a tiny flower vase to display a wild riverside beauty at the table. We bring hot soups, but we also adore our recipe for a tomato bread soup that is best served cold (see page 144). It is a refreshing appetizer to a campsite meal. The sound of rushing water and the sway of the birch trees, and sometimes cottonwood trees mixed in, makes the setting always lively and festive. Sharing a meal with our guests along a wild river is a true movable feast.

And, south of the million-acre backyard of Winterlake Lodge, we prepare lunches for our guests who are traveling to see and photograph bears and other animals such as wolves in the wilderness of Katmai National Park and Preserve. All of our guests at Tutka Bay Lodge have the option to spend a day flying to a remarkable location by small plane and returning to the lodge in the late afternoon. We often join the expedition as something like in-field caterers. The wild plants, flowers, salmon, and sea life are so abundant, no wonder brown bears congregate here to feast. The people at Katmai National Park and Preserve post photos on Facebook of various bears they observe through the summer. Each fall, they have a contest called "Fat Bear Week" where viewers can vote on what bear became the fattest. It's hilarious. We Alaskans, bears and humans, know how to eat well within the wild.

WILD BREAD

We take these savory breads, wrapped in aluminum foil, to heat over campfires along the river or down by the sea. They are delicious either hot or cold. We learned this recipe from our Moroccan chef-friend, Hicham Hnini. Imagine all the delicious fillings Hicham creates—or, the delicious fillings you can create.

MAKES 4 SERVINGS

FOR THE BREAD
2 teaspoons active dry yeast
1 tablespoon sugar
2 cups water, warmed to 105°F
3½ cups all-purpose flour, plus more for dusting
½ cup whole wheat flour
½ tablespoon sea salt

FOR THE FILLING
1 teaspoon extra-virgin olive oil
1 teaspoon unsalted butter
1 yellow onion, sliced
1 red apple, cored and thinly sliced
1 small bunch Swiss chard, stemmed and diced
1 cup shredded white cheddar cheese
Canola oil for greasing

In a bowl, mix the yeast, sugar, and warm water. Let the mixture stand for 5 minutes. In another bowl, mix the flours and salt. Add the yeast mixture and mix until a ball is formed. Knead the dough with your hands on a lightly floured work surface until a smooth elastic ball is formed, 10 to 15 minutes. Cover with a damp kitchen towel and let rest for 20 minutes.

To make the filling, in a sauté pan over medium-low heat, warm the oil and butter. Add the onion and apple and sauté until the onion and apple are soft and caramelized, about 20 minutes. Remove from the heat. Add the chard and cheese and mix well, sprinkling in a bit of water if necessary, to loosen the mixture.

Divide the dough into 4 equal balls. Roll out 1 ball to a 6-by-8-inch rectangle that's about ¼ inch thick. Place ½ cup of the filling down a line in the center of the dough. Fold a long edge of the dough over the filling. Repeat the fold on the other side. Pinch the edges of the dough in the center together and seal completely. Gently roll the filled dough flat again, starting from one short end to the other, being careful to not tear any edges. Repeat to roll and fill the remaining 3 dough pieces.

Heat a cast-iron skillet over medium-low heat and brush with oil. Place the breads into the skillet without crowding. Cook until the dough is golden on the bottom and beginning to puff, about 5 minutes. Flip the bread over and cook the other side until golden, about 5 more minutes. Transfer to a plate. Repeat until all breads are cooked. Cut the breads into 2-inch slices and serve warm.

TOMATO BREAD SOUP

This soup recipe, our take on a classic Spanish salmorejo, is a popular one in our cooking classes. We love the cool, refreshing flavor packed in a thermos when we are out hiking. Because it isn't served hot (although we suppose it could be) we don't have to fuss about temperatures. The flavor is a knock-out, even for people who don't care for "tomato soup." We prepare this Spanish specialty "Alaska-style" by adding salmon bacon and big, crispy Alaska sourdough croutons.

MAKES 4 TO 6 SERVINGS

2 quarts water

2 pounds good-quality fresh ripe tomatoes

2 cloves garlic

½ pound sourdough bread, torn and toasted

¼ cup extra-virgin olive oil, plus
    more as needed

Sea salt

Splash of sherry vinegar

4 to 6 slices Rhubarb Salmon Bacon
    (page 40), torn into pieces

4 to 6 slices sourdough bread,
    crust removed and torn into pieces

In a saucepan, bring the water to a boil over high heat. Using a small knife, cut and X in the flesh on the bottom of each tomato (this makes removing the skin much easier). Plunge the tomatoes, a few at a time, into the boiling water and blanch them to loosen the skin, about 30 seconds.

Remove the tomatoes from the water and let cool slightly. Using your fingers or a paring knife, peel away and discard the tomato skins, starting at the X.

Quarter the peeled tomatoes, then put them into a blender. Add the garlic cloves. Soak the toasted bread in water for a few seconds, squeeze it with your hands, and add it to the blender with the tomatoes and garlic. Puree until the mixture is smooth, about 2 minutes.

While the blender is running, drizzle in the oil until incorporated. Add salt to taste and the vinegar and blend for 10 more seconds. Pour the soup into a bowl and refrigerate for at least 2 hours before serving.

Meanwhile, make the croutons: In a sauté pan over medium heat, warm 3 tablespoons olive oil. When hot, add the sourdough bread pieces. Toss the bread continuously until the bread is toasted and golden brown, about 5 minutes. Season lightly with salt. Set aside on a paper towel.

To serve, ladle the soup into serving bowls. Top each with a few pieces of salmon bacon, croutons, and a drizzle of extra-virgin olive oil.

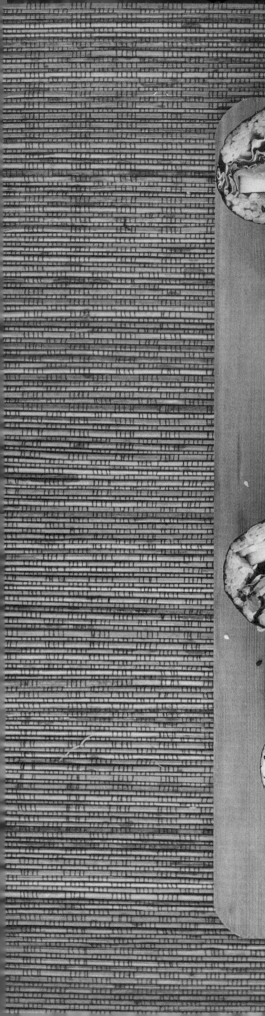

SMOKED SALMON & VEGETABLE RICE SANDWICHES

These sandwiches are called onigirazu in Japanese and they are one of our all-time favorites for guests out on the trail or on the mountain. The nori sheet is laid out in a diamond shape and the rice is a square right in the center so the points of nori will fold over it. Black garlic can be purchased at any Asian market.

MAKES 4 SANDWICHES

1 cucumber, peeled and thinly sliced

1 carrot, peeled and julienned

4 leaves Napa cabbage, shredded

6 cups water, plus more as needed

½ cup plus 2 tablespoons rice vinegar

¼ cup plus 2 teaspoons sugar

2 cups short-grain sushi rice

4 tablespoons mayonnaise

1 tablespoon sweet soy sauce

1 teaspoon pureed black garlic

2 tablespoons sesame seeds, toasted

4 sheets sushi nori

12 (1-ounce) slices cold-smoked salmon (lox)

Put the cucumber, carrot, and cabbage into separate bowls. In a liquid measuring cup with a spout, mix together 3 cups of the water, ½ cup of the rice vinegar, and ¼ cup of the sugar. Divide this mixture among the bowls. Cover the bowls with clean kitchen towels. Refrigerate the vegetables overnight.

Put the rice into a bowl and add room temperature water to cover. Move the rice around with your fingers to release the starches, then drain through a fine mesh sieve. Repeat 3 more times until water is fairly clear.

Put the rice into a small saucepan, add the remaining 3 cups water and cover with a lid. Bring the water to a boil over high heat. Reduce the heat to medium-low and cook until the water is absorbed, about 20 minutes. Turn off the heat and keep the lid on for another 10 minutes.

While the rice cooks, mix together the remaining 2 tablespoons vinegar and 2 teaspoons sugar until the sugar dissolves. Once the rice is ready, transfer it to bowl and sprinkle the vinegar-sugar mixture onto the warm rice while gently mixing with a spatula or wooden spoon until the rice is coated. Let the rice cool to room temperature, then cover it with a clean, damp kitchen towel.

In a bowl, mix together the mayonnaise, soy sauce, and black garlic. Pull the vegetables out of their pickling liquids and drain on paper towels.

Continued on page 148

...CONTINUED
SMOKED SALMON & VEGETABLE RICE SANDWICHES

With moistened hands, take about ½ cup of the rice and form it into a small, squared cake. Continue to make 8 rice cakes total. Sprinkle each cake with ½ tablespoon of toasted sesame seeds. Arrange the nori sheets on a work surface with one of the corners pointed towards you. Place 1 rice cake into the center of each nori sheet, counter to the pointed corners. For each sandwich, spread about 1 tablespoon of the mayonnaise mixture on the rice and then layer 3 slices of smoked salmon on top. Next, add some carrot, some cucumber, and some of the cabbage. Top with another rice cake and press down to compress the ingredients.

Fold the corners of the nori sheet to the center of the sandwich to create a sealed bundle. Wrap the sandwich tightly in Bee's Wrap or another non-plastic wrap to seal well.

To serve, remove the Bee's Wrap and cut the bundles in half.

POTATO & SMOKED CHERRY SALAD

This recipe was inspired by the Alaska wildfires in the summer of 2019. Interestingly, the cherries on our tree retained a smoked flavor at the end of that summer season. The wildfires were devastating, but the cherries gave us some new flavor ideas.

MAKES 4 TO 6 SERVINGS

3 tablespoons alder wood chips

10 small Yukon gold potatoes, boiled until tender and cooled

1 cup fresh sour red cherries

½ red onion

5 green onions

½ cup minced fresh flat-leaf parsley

6 slices bacon, cooked crisp and cooled

½ cup dried cranberries

1 cup shredded Manchego cheese

4 hard-boiled eggs, peeled and quartered

¼ cup red wine vinegar

1 cup mayonnaise

½ cup Greek-style plain yogurt

½ teaspoon Dijon mustard

2 teaspoons hot pepper sauce

Sea salt and freshly ground black pepper

In a 6-quart casserole with a tight-fitting lid, fit a piece of aluminum foil into the bottom of the pot. Place the wood chips over the foil. Place an additional piece of foil over the wood chips. Turn on your kitchen ventilation. Heat the pot on the stove top over medium heat until the wood chips are smoking, about 5 minutes. Place a steamer or rack that fits into the pot on top of the foil. Cut the potatoes into 1-inch cubes and place them onto the steamer or rack. Add the cherries to pot with the potatoes. Cover the pot and turn the heat off. Let the potatoes and cherries absorb the smoke for about 30 minutes.

While the potatoes and cherries are smoking, cut the red onion into small dice. Place the onion into a large bowl. Slice the green onions and add about three-fifths of them to the bowl along with the parsley. Chop the bacon and set aside.

Remove the potato-cherry mixture from the smoker. Cut the cherries in half and remove any pits. Place into the bowl with the onions and parsley. Add the chopped bacon, dried cranberries, cheese, and hard-boiled eggs. Gently stir in the vinegar, mayonnaise, yogurt, mustard, pepper sauce, and plenty of salt and pepper to taste. Mix thoroughly. Serve garnished with the remaining sliced green onions.

PAN-SEARED CHICKEN & MINT FRESH ROLLS

We love this unique fresh roll recipe and want to share it with you. What makes it special is the grilled hot chicken in the center of the roll, wrapped around the aromatic herbs and fresh greens. Try it with other savory hot center items, like fish or beef.

MAKES 6 ROLLS

1 (8-ounce) package dried rice vermicelli noodles

Boiling water

4 teaspoons toasted sesame oil

1 boneless, skinless chicken breast half, cut into thin slices

5 tablespoons canola oil

4 tablespoons soy sauce

3 cloves garlic, minced

1 small knob ginger, peeled and minced

1 teaspoon sugar

Juice of ½ lime

2 green onions, finely sliced

6 Vietnamese rice paper rounds, 8½-inches in diameter

2 cups baby spinach

2 carrots, peeled and cut into thin strips

½ cup roughly chopped fresh cilantro

½ cup roughly chopped fresh mint

Cashew Sauce (page 288) (optional)

Place the noodles in a heatproof bowl and cover with boiling water. Add 2 teaspoons of the sesame oil and let the noodles stand for about 10 minutes. Drain the noodles and refrigerate to chill.

In a bowl, combine the sliced chicken, 3 tablespoons of the canola oil, 3 tablespoons of the soy sauce, the remaining 2 teaspoons sesame oil, minced garlic, and ginger. Toss to coat the chicken well and refrigerate for 20 minutes. Toss the chilled noodles with the sugar, the remaining 1 tablespoon soy sauce, the lime juice, and green onions. Set aside.

Remove the chicken from the marinade with tongs, letting any excess liquid drip away. Heat a sauté pan over medium heat and add the remaining 2 tablespoons canola oil. Add the chicken and sauté until firm and golden brown, 3 to 4 minutes per side. Turn the heat off and keep the chicken warm.

Fill a shallow dish with warm water. Soak 1 rice paper sheet in the water until pliable, 5 to 10 seconds. Remove the rice paper and carefully place onto a flat work surface. Layer some of the rice noodle mixture, spinach, carrots, cilantro, and mint in the center of the paper. Be careful not to overfill. Repeat with the remaining wrappers, spacing them apart on the work surface. Once all the wrappers are piled with the vegetables, divide the warm chicken on top of the piles. For each roll, fold opposite sides of the rice paper to the center and then roll up the paper around the filling as tightly as you can without tearing it.

Cut the fresh rolls on the diagonal and serve right away with the Cashew Sauce for dipping, if desired.

RASPBERRY-CHOCOLATE CHIP COOKIES

Everyone needs a foolproof chocolate chip cookie recipe, and this one has a special fruity surprise. These are beloved cookies from Mandy's childhood. The chip-to-dough ratio is key, according to our cookie-tasting experts Carl and Mandy.

MAKES 16 COOKIES

⅓ cup raspberry preserves

2½ cups all-purpose flour

2 teaspoons sea salt

1 teaspoon baking soda

½ teaspoon baking powder

1 cup unsalted butter,
   at room temperature

1 cup packed light brown sugar

½ cup granulated sugar

2 large eggs

2 teaspoons pure vanilla bean paste
   or vanilla extract

2½ cups semisweet chocolate chips

Line two 13-by-18-inch baking sheets with parchment paper or silicone baking mats.

Scoop the raspberry preserves into teaspoon-size balls and place them 1 inch apart on one of the baking sheets. Freeze the balls until they are firm and easy to pick up, 1 to 2 hours or preferably overnight. Keep frozen until ready to use.

In a bowl, mix together the flour, salt, baking soda, and baking powder. In the bowl of a stand mixer fitted with the paddle attachment, whip the butter and both sugars until light and fluffy, about 2 minutes. Stop the mixer and scrape down the sides of the bowl. Add the eggs and vanilla and mix until incorporated. Scrape down the bowl again. Add the flour mixture and mix until incorporated. Mix in the chocolate chips.

Scoop 1 tablespoon of the dough onto the second lined baking sheet. Put a frozen preserves ball on top of the dough and then top it with another tablespoon of cookie dough, rolling the dough to completely encase the preserves. Continue until all the cookie dough and preserves balls are used, spacing the cookies 2 inches apart on the pan. Chill the filled cookies for 20 minutes. Meanwhile, preheat the oven to 325°F.

Pull the cookies out of the refrigerator, press down on them lightly to flatten them, and place in the oven. Bake until the cookies are light golden brown, 7 to 8 minutes, rotating the cookies halfway through. Cool the cookies slightly. Serve warm.

BIRDSEED BARS

We love these bars. They hold up well in packaged lunches and are always a favorite at the coffee bar. We change the seed mixtures and ratios from time to time, as can you, but it is important to keep the chia and flaxseed in the mix. We use birch syrup, an Alaska staple that we tap from our own trees in spring, but you can also use maple syrup or another favorite syrup here. Birch syrup is available through online sources.

MAKES 8 BARS

Canola oil for greasing
¾ cup birch syrup or other syrup
½ cup sesame seeds
¼ cup shelled pumpkin seeds
 (pepitas)
½ cup shelled sunflower seeds

¼ cup chia seeds
¼ cup hemp seeds
½ cup wheat bran
½ cup ground flaxseed
¼ teaspoon sea salt

Preheat the oven to 325°F. Grease a piece of parchment paper to fit inside an 8-by-8-inch baking pan.

In a small saucepan over low heat, heat the syrup until warmed through, about 2 minutes; this will help it to mix more easily. In a bowl, combine the sesame seeds, pumpkin seeds, sunflower seeds, chia seeds, hemp seeds, wheat bran, flaxseed, and salt and mix well. Add the warmed syrup and mix until well incorporated.

Pour the seed mixture into the prepared pan and spread it out into an even layer. Put a second sheet of greased parchment paper (greased-side down) directly on top of the mixture. Press down with your hands or another pan to compress the mixture into an even layer. Remove top layer of parchment before baking.

Put the pan into the oven for 20 minutes, then rotate the pan 90 degrees and bake until golden brown, another 20 minutes. At this point the bars will have a chewy consistency. If you prefer your bars to have a crunchy texture, bake them for another 5 to 10 minutes.

Pull the pan out of oven and set on a wire rack to cool completely. When cool, cut the bar into 2-by-4-inch bars (or into the desired size) and store in an airtight container. The bars will keep for up to 7 days.

BLUEBERRY SEAWEED LEATHER

We've been making fruit leathers from wild Alaska berries since the girls were little. This version adds flaked seaweed, which adds a little savory note. Let's face it, seaweed goes well with everything!

MAKES 6 SERVINGS

Canola oil for greasing, if needed

4 cups fresh blueberries

2 tablespoons sugar

1 teaspoon sea salt

1 tablespoon fresh lemon juice

¼ cup dehydrated seaweed, flaked

Preheat the oven to as low as it will go, ideally 200°F. Line a 13-by-18-inch baking sheet with a silicone baking mat or greased parchment paper.

In a saucepan, combine the berries, sugar, and salt and bring to a simmer over medium-high heat. Reduce the heat to low and simmer until the fruit is very soft, 10 to 15 minutes. Remove from the heat. Add the lemon juice and mix well. Transfer the berry mixture to a blender and puree until smooth.

Pour the puree onto the prepared baking sheet; the mixture should be about ¼-inch thick. Sprinkle the top evenly with the flaked seaweed.

Put the pan into the oven and turn on the convection fan, if you have one. Bake until the fruit mixture is dried but slightly pliable, 4 to 6 hours, depending on the moisture in the berries.

Remove the dried fruit leather from the oven and cut it into six 3-inch strips along the long side of the pan. Roll up each piece of fruit leather. Store the fruit leather in an airtight container and wrap in parchment to transport. If you like, tie each roll with butcher's twine. The fruit leather will last for 1 week.

LEMON HONEY CAKE WITH RICOTTA

We make homemade ricotta at our cooking school using lemons for the acid component, so it seems like ricotta always goes naturally well with lemons. This is the perfect cozy companion for tea (which Kirsten prefers over coffee) sitting at the small table near the garden.

MAKES 10 TO 12 SERVINGS

½ cup unsalted butter, at room temperature, plus more for buttering the pan

Canola oil for greasing

1½ cups all-purpose flour

2 teaspoons baking powder

½ teaspoon sea salt

½ cup sugar

½ cup honey

2 tablespoons finely grated lemon zest

2 tablespoons fresh lemon juice

1 tablespoon lemon thyme leaves

3 large eggs

1 teaspoon pure vanilla bean paste or vanilla extract

1½ cups whole-milk ricotta cheese

Preheat the oven to 350°F. Grease an 8-inch round cake pan and line it with buttered parchment paper.

In a bowl, whisk together the flour, baking powder, and salt. In the bowl of a stand mixer fitted with the paddle attachment, combine the sugar, honey, ½ cup butter, lemon zest, lemon juice, and lemon thyme. Beat until the mixture is pale and fluffy, about 2 minutes. While beating, add the eggs one at a time and then beat in the vanilla. Add half of the flour mixture and the ricotta and mix until just combined. Using a rubber spatula, gently fold the rest of the flour mixture into the batter, taking care to ensure the ingredients are evenly incorporated.

Pour the batter into the prepared pan and spread into an even layer. Bake until the cake is lightly golden, firm, and a cake tester inserted into the center comes out clean, about 50 minutes.

Let the cake cool in the pan for about 10 minutes. To unmold, invert the cake onto a plate, remove the pan, and peel off the parchment paper.

To serve, cut the cake into wedges and serve on plates slightly warm or at room temperature.

SMOKY BLUEBERRY-BACON MELTS

These are best served hot with a big, refreshing mixed-green salad and a platter of just-baked cookies, but they are good out in the field as well. They are a pick-me-up after a morning of skiing in the winter or river rafting in the summer. We like the blueberry jam to have bits of blueberries for texture. We make our own wild-gathered blueberry jams and syrups.

MAKES 4 SANDWICHES

8 strips smoked bacon

¼ cup Blueberry Syrup (page 287)

8 tablespoons unsalted butter

1 yellow onion, halved and thinly sliced

Leaves from 4 sprigs fresh thyme

4 tablespoons mayonnaise

8 thick slices sourdough bread

8 slices sharp cheddar cheese

8 tablespoons blueberry jam

¼ cup arugula leaves

Rice wine vinegar

Sea salt and freshly ground black pepper

Preheat the oven to 400°F. Line a baking sheet with parchment paper.

Place the bacon on the prepared baking sheet in a single layer and bake until medium crisp, about 13 minutes. Remove the bacon from the oven and brush with some of the syrup. Continue to bake the bacon until crisp, about 5 more minutes.

Melt 2 tablespoons of the butter in a sauté pan over low heat. Add the onion and cook until it begins to caramelize and color, about 8 minutes. Add the thyme leaves. Remove from the heat.

Spread 1 tablespoon of the mayonnaise on one side of 4 slices of bread and then top with 1 slice of cheese and spread with 2 tablespoons of the jam. On the other slices of bread, place 1 slice of the cheese and top with 2 slices of bacon and

2 tablespoons of the caramelized onions. Place the mayonnaise-jam-cheese-topped bread slices on top of the bacon-onion-topped bread slices, lining up the edges, and lightly press together.

Heat a sauté pan over low heat. Using half of the remaining butter, butter the tops of the sandwiches and place in the hot pan, butter side down. Then, butter the other sides of the sandwiches. Fry the sandwiches until golden, about 2 minutes, then flip them and fry the other side in the same manner. Use a metal spatula to gently press down on the bread to encourage browning.

In a bowl, toss the arugula with some vinegar. Season lightly with salt and pepper. Insert some of the arugula into each sandwich. Halve the sandwiches and serve warm.

HIGH TUNNEL VEGGIE SANDWICH

We have fun thinking about creative lunches for guests on the go. We often mix up vegetarian and meat-lover's options, so we aren't falling into the old bagged sandwich routine. We think that healthy vegetable sandwiches provide a nice clean energy for guests breathing in all of our wild and rarified air.

MAKES 2 SANDWICHES

1 carrot, peeled and diced

2 small red radishes, quartered

½ red onion, chopped

1 small bunch fresh flat-leaf parsley

4 large fresh basil leaves

1 tablespoon fresh tarragon leaves

1 tablespoon minced fresh chives

2 cloves garlic

1 tablespoon mild miso paste

8 ounces cream cheese

2 teaspoons tomato paste

Sea salt and freshly ground black pepper

2 tablespoons canola oil

½ zucchini, sliced

½ yellow squash, sliced

2 hoagie-size sourdough baguettes, cut in half lengthwise

¼ cup shelled sunflower seeds

2 cups baby spinach leaves

1 cucumber, peeled and thinly sliced

½ green apple, thinly sliced

1 large green or red tomato, thickly sliced

1 cup broccoli or other sprouts

Put the carrot and radishes in a food processor and process until a chunky puree forms. Add the red onion, parsley, basil, tarragon, chives, garlic, and miso. Process until the mixture is well mixed. Add the cream cheese and tomato paste and process until smooth. Season to taste with salt and pepper.

Heat a sauté pan over high heat. When hot, reduce the heat to medium and add the oil, zucchini, and yellow squash. Sauté the vegetables until golden brown and caramelized, about 6 minutes. Remove from the pan and set aside to cool.

When you're ready to serve, spread a good amount of the cream cheese mixture on the top and bottom sides of the baguettes. Sprinkle the sunflower seeds onto the cream cheese spread, dividing evenly. Layer the spinach, cucumber, apple, tomato, and sprouts over the cream cheese mixture, seasoning lightly with salt and pepper as you layer. Serve immediately or wrap the sandwich in Bee's Wrap or another non-plastic wrap to serve in the field.

A FISHER, A MUSHER, A KING

In all the years of living the Alaska lodge-life, we have met the most remarkable people from around the world. And, as the title of this chapter implies, people from all types of backgrounds.

Our company mission statement says that we wish to provide our guests with the opportunity to experience the powerful sense of time spent in the natural world, to experience new and enriching adventures that become lifetime memories, and to bring individuals and families closer together in a creative and positive environment. We've learned to better understand the human condition, certainly, as well as experience diverse family and cultural dynamics. We are always amazed at how we, our small family, have been given the opportunity to host guests from far-flung places, these people who have found their way to our corner of the world, to our small lodges, and to our tables.

All the people who enter our lives leave small (and sometimes not so small) imprints of themselves upon us. And, we hope we can share our honest and authentic thoughts and feelings with them as well—like, how it makes us feel to stand on an unnamed mountain or breathe crisp glacier air, or to look down and find an ancient rock on a beach that will become a treasured keepsake. We work hard at this connection and relationship through the orchestration of our food—through presentation and style of flavors and textures; dishware; music; just-picked fresh flowers—whatever little things are that we can do to make the setting more beautiful.

It's appetizer hour at Winterlake Lodge. Our guests gather together in the bar before dinner, where we offer an ever-changing collection of appetizers and wines. It starts with selecting the music and then a check of the lights. The bar is set with wildflowers picked from the meadow or swaths of just-cut black currant branches woven around platters of hot and cold hors d'oeuvres, small plates, and stacks of little napkins. White scentless candles are lit and tucked around. And then, the guests begin to wander in, animated from their day of adventure, animal sightings, glacier trekking, or fly fishing. It's a festive moment we never get tired of. Then Mandy walks through the velvet curtains between the kitchen and the bar. She is deftly carrying a black wok filled with Chinese-style scallops. The smell of the scallops penetrates the most intent of conversations, and guests begin to gather around. Mandy sets down the scallops next to a piece of glacial slate that Carl brought down from one of his mountain trips. It's piled high with small triangular just-fried rice cakes. Next comes out a tray of halibut dolloped with chutney along with the nightly cheese selection and homemade crackers. Wine is poured, and the sound of happy voices, happy people, fill the lodge.

> All the people who enter our lives leave small (and sometimes not so small) imprints of themselves upon us.

These are the rules of our bar appetizer hour: Make our humble lodge as convivial as possible. Be as present and focused on these guests at this moment as we can. Be generous and gracious.

We seat guests together to encourage community and communication, to share and discover what common bonds even strangers might find through traveling. There have been many remarkable conversations at our table.

One year, Kirsten's father, Jim Schmidt, a decorated war hero, was visiting Winterlake Lodge for a few days. There was a group of guests at the lodge there to fly-fish for salmon.

The guests were from the German lake district of Lake Constance. As they sat together at the dinner table, after a bit of small talk, the question was asked, as it might always be between older German and American men—were you in the war? Jim easily rattled off dates and places from World War II battles he hadn't mentioned before or since, places so embedded in his memory, they resurfaced effortlessly. The German men told Jim they had all fought together in a same battle as he. What were the odds of these old men coming together, here in Alaska at our table? They shared the camaraderie of luck and survival. The men talked together long into the night.

These are moments we treasure.

Another summer, at Tutka Bay Lodge, Carly invited Homer-based anthropologist Nancy Klein to join her to dine with archeologists visiting from New York City. Nancy brought along a friend of hers named Pete Zollars. Pete shared the story about how he worked at Tutka Bay Lodge in the 1970s and excavated a native hearth, the term for a cooking surface area carved out from rock, that carbon-dated back a thousand years ago. The knowledge of such a unique artifact of history hidden on our property would have never been known to us if Carly hadn't invited Nancy to dinner. And if Nancy hadn't brought along Pete with her, and if the conversation hadn't led to that subject, we might never have discovered the hearth. The fact that we have a 1,000-year-old native hearth has totally ignited our imaginations, enriched our lives, and it's made a difference.

There are many conversations and stories, moments of amazement and laughter we've had at our tables over the years. These are moments we treasure. People being happy at the table, eating food they enjoy, the perfect moments they spend with companions, make the hard work of culinary life rewarding.

We have had many favorite guest moments centered around food. We laugh at the memory of a prominent Russian family who came to stay with us in the winter at Winterlake Lodge. They asked to have a barbecue in the front yard off the big deck even though it was in February. We shoveled out the grill from under (many) feet of snow and loaded it up with alder wood. We grilled reindeer and vegetables over the live fire, and we played Russian music over a wireless speaker. We all drank vodka and danced on the deck until late into the night. The joy our Russian guests had for snow and the cold, for the darkness of winter and the clean air and life itself, was infectious.

And the Indian family that brought their own chef along to prepare Southern Indian cuisine. We decided we wanted to cook for the family as well, so we compromised on a fifty-fifty split of the table, half lodge-based dishes and half Indian food. We served all in a sort of wedding-feast style with small platters passed around the table, being shared, and all the dishes being tried. It felt like a true feast.

Or, the time we had a group of fifteen chefs and culinary professionals at the lodge. As we sat down to dinner, different chefs jumped up and wanted to prepare something else for the table. We lost count of the courses we had. The energy we all had for cooking, even though we went late into the night, is still a fond memory. We had three different desserts!

Sometimes, particularly in the winter, by candlelight, Carl reads poetry just as guests have finished dinner, over an evening coffee or wine. A favorite poet of Carl's is Robert Service. Service's poetry brings to life the rough and tumble days of gold mining and how such a wild place made him feel.

SIZZLING SAKE YUZU DUMPLINGS

These appetizers are aromatic, dramatic, and delicious. We serve these on oven- or campfire-heated stones that make the sauce sizzle. We prefer to use sweet Alaska shrimp in our dumplings rather than the pork you find in typical Chinese dumplings. Sake is a favorite cooking alcohol that offers a sweet, yeasty flavor.

MAKES 4 SERVINGS

FOR THE FILLING

1 cup spot shrimp

2 large leaves Napa cabbage,
   hard stem removed, shredded

4 green onions, finely chopped

2 cloves garlic, minced

1-inch knob ginger, peeled and minced

1 tablespoon soy sauce

1 tablespoon toasted sesame oil

1 teaspoon hot pepper sauce

Sea salt

FOR THE SAKE-YUZU SAUCE

2 tablespoons soy sauce

1 tablespoon rice vinegar

2 teaspoons toasted sesame oil

2 tablespoons yuzu juice

2 tablespoon sake

2 teaspoons canola oil

2 tablespoons cornstarch

24 homemade Dumpling Wrappers
   (page 289) or store-bought

4 tablespoons canola oil

To make the filling, in a food processor, pulse the shrimp until finely minced but not yet a paste. In a large bowl, combine the cabbage, green onions, garlic, ginger, soy sauce, sesame oil, pepper sauce, and a pinch of salt and mix well. Add the pureed shrimp and mix well. Cover with a kitchen towel until ready to use.

To make the sauce, in a bowl, mix together the soy sauce, vinegar, sesame oil, yuzu juice, sake, and oil. Set aside.

To make the dumplings, sprinkle the cornstarch onto a tray. Have a small bowl of warm water and a kettle of hot water nearby. Hold a dumpling wrapper in the palm of one hand, and put a heaped teaspoon of the filling onto the center of the wrapper. Dip your finger in the warm water and wipe around the edge of the wrapper. Bring the edges of the wrapper together. Pinch pleats along one side, then press each pleat against the opposite flat side of the wrapper. As you work, put each dumpling onto the tray. Continue to assemble with the remaining wrappers and filling.

Heat a large nonstick sauté pan over medium heat and add 1 tablespoon of oil. Brush off any excess cornstarch from the dumplings. Add 6 dumplings to the pan and fry until golden brown, about 1½ minutes. Add a splash of water to the pan and cover with a lid. Cook until the water has evaporated and the filling is cooked through, 3 to 5 minutes. Add 2 tablespoons of the sake-yuzu sauce and toss to coat. Transfer the steamed dumplings to a serving tray and serve immediately. Wipe out the pan with paper towels and continue to cook the remaining dumplings in the same manner in 3 batches. Serve right away.

SMOKED SALMON CARDAMOM SPREAD

The flavors of sour cream (rather than cream cheese), lemon, and pepper compliment salmon perfectly. We pair this aromatic spread with our Seed Crackers (page 176), use it as a filling in our Wild Bread (page 143), or spread it on omelets. The recipe was a happy accident many years ago and it is still a favorite.

MAKES 24 (1-OUNCE) SERVINGS

1 pound hot smoked (kippered) salmon

¾ cup sour cream

½ teaspoon ground cardamom

Freshly ground black pepper

Juice of 1 lemon

Put half the kippered salmon in the bowl of a food processor and process until chopped. Add the sour cream, cardamom, and pepper to taste. Add the lemon juice. Process the salmon mixture until it is pureed. Transfer the puree to a large bowl.

Coarsely chop the remaining salmon and add it to the puree. Mix well, cover, and refrigerate until serving time.

GINGER HALIBUT CAKES

Halibut cakes are always delicious, but they sing with the sweet and sour notes of our Rhubarb Chutney (page 291). Luckily for us, Tutka Bay Lodge is located in Kachemak Bay, the halibut capital of the world. This recipe is specifically for leftover cooked fish so nothing is ever wasted. Serve these for lunch with a salad, as a beef burger substitute, or as little bites at appetizer hour.

MAKES 4 SERVINGS

1 pound halibut fillet, cooked, cooled, and flaked

¼ cup sliced green onions

Juice of 1 lemon

½ cup breadcrumbs

¼ cup chopped fresh cilantro

¾ cup mayonnaise

1 large egg

1 teaspoon hot pepper sauce

2 cloves garlic, minced

1-inch knob fresh ginger, peeled and grated

Sea salt and freshly ground black pepper

1 teaspoon canola oil

1 teaspoon unsalted butter

Rhubarb Chutney (page 291)

To make the halibut cakes, in a large bowl, combine the halibut, green onions, lemon juice, breadcrumbs, cilantro, mayonnaise, egg, hot pepper sauce, garlic, and ginger until well blended. Season with salt and pepper to taste. The mixture should be moist enough to form small patties and hold together.

Divide the mixture into 4 equal portions. With moistened hands, pat out the portions into round patties. Lay the formed patties onto a greased, parchment-lined baking sheet.

Heat a large sauté pan over medium-low heat and add the oil and butter. When the butter melts, add the fish cakes and sauté until firm and golden, about 2 minutes. Turn over the cakes and sauté until the other side is firm, about 2 minutes more. Transfer the fish cakes to paper towels to drain and keep warm.

Serve the halibut cakes warm with a dollop of chutney on top.

SEED CRACKERS

If you've been thumbing through the recipes in this book, by now you might notice a theme: We love seeds in everything. Seed varieties line our shelves and we use them in just about every kind of dish. (Perhaps we have been living amongst birds too long.) These crackers are so delicious, we have made them a staple item in our lodge kitchens.

MAKES ABOUT 9 LARGE CRACKERS

Canola oil for greasing
¾ cup water, plus more if needed
¼ cup honey
1 cup whole flaxseeds
1 cup chia seeds

1 cup shelled sunflower seeds
1 cup shelled pumpkin seeds (pepitas)
½ cup sesame seeds, toasted
1 tablespoon dried flaked seaweed
1 teaspoon sea salt

Preheat the oven to 225°F. Line a baking sheet with parchment paper and lightly grease with canola oil.

Mix together the water and honey. Add the flaxseed and chia seeds and allow to soak and plump for about 5 minutes. Stir in the sunflower seeds, pumpkin seeds, sesame seeds, flaked seaweed, and salt, adding a bit more water if the mixture is a little dry. With moistened hands, pat the seed mixture onto the baking sheet, compressing the mixture slightly until it is about ¼-inch thick. Bake for 1 hour. Check the pan from time to time in case the oven is cooking unevenly, rotating the pan as necessary. If the seeds are crisp, remove from the oven. If the seeds are still pliable, bake them for an additional 5 to 10 minutes, checking closely.

Cool the crackers and break them up into approximately 4-inch shards or cut them into neat squares. Store them in an airtight container. The crackers will remain fresh for 1 week.

OYSTER POTATO TARTLETS

We believe that winter is a time to indulge and dine on richer, heartier foods, like these miniature oyster tarts. But we love oysters any time of year. Do you ever want a little bite of oyster and not a big raw thing? This is just the right celebratory taste when we are in that mood.

MAKES 4 ENTRÉE SERVINGS OR 8 APPETIZER SERVINGS

Canola oil

4 cups shredded uncooked Yukon Gold potatoes

Sea salt and freshly ground black pepper

1 egg white

½ yellow onion, finely diced

1 clove garlic, minced

2 tablespoons unsalted butter

1 leek, white part only, thinly sliced

1 small fennel bulb, trimmed and thinly sliced

2 teaspoons fennel seeds

1 cup store-bought or homemade chicken stock

1 cup heavy cream

1 dozen small oysters, shucked, juices reserved

¼ cup Parmigiano-Reggiano cheese

Preheat the oven to 400°F. Grease four 4-inch tart pans.

Rinse the potatoes under cold water and squeeze, using your hands to press out the excess water. Sprinkle liberally with salt and toss well. Place the potatoes in a lightly moistened cheesecloth and squeeze out some of the potato starch and liquid. Place the potatoes in a colander to drain for 15 minutes.

In a bowl, mix the egg white, onion, and garlic. Add the shredded potato and mix thoroughly. Press the potato mixture into the tart pans, dividing evenly and pressing against the pan firmly. Season lightly with salt and pepper and brush lightly with oil. There should be some potato mixture remaining. Set aside. Bake the tart shells on the center rack of the oven for 30 minutes.

Remove from the oven and reduce the oven heat to 350°F.

Place a 4-quart high-sided sauté pan over medium-high heat and add the butter, leek, fennel, and fennel seed, seasoning with a bit more salt and pepper; cook, stirring, for 1 to 2 minutes. Add the chicken stock and heavy cream, bringing to a simmer. Cook until the liquid is reduced by half, about 10 minutes. Add the oysters and oyster juices, cook for 1 minute, then remove from heat.

Divide the oyster mixture among the tart shells. Top with any additional shredded potato mixture and the Parmigiano-Reggiano cheese. Place the tartlets back into the oven and cook until the top crust is a golden brown, about 10 to 12 minutes.

Serve warm.

CHILE SCALLOPS

We dream of someday going to Singapore in the off-season and setting up a hawker stand to sell Alaska seafood dishes. There, we might serve this dish, which has the same basic sauce and technique we use for our chile crab. We serve these scallops with hot, fluffy short-grain white rice. If you like, top servings with thinly sliced fresh red chiles.

MAKES 4 SERVINGS

¼ cup chile garlic sauce

1 cup canned tomato sauce

½ cup store-bought or homemade chicken stock

½ cup dry sherry

2 tablespoons sugar

2 tablespoons cornstarch

3 tablespoons cold water

¼ cup canola oil

12 large scallops, side muscles removed

Sea salt and freshly ground black pepper

1 clove garlic, minced

1 small shallot, minced

1 small knob fresh ginger, peeled and grated

1 teaspoon toasted sesame oil

¼ cup small fresh cilantro leaves

In a bowl, mix together the chile with garlic sauce, tomato sauce, chicken stock, sherry, and sugar. In a small bowl, whisk together the cornstarch and water until dissolved.

Put a large wok (or a cast-iron skillet) on the stove top over medium-high heat. When the wok is hot, add the canola oil and swirl to coat the bottom of the pan. Pat the scallops completely dry with paper towels. Season with salt and pepper. Add the seasoned scallops to the wok and cook undisturbed so they develop a crust and caramelize, about 2 minutes. Add the garlic, shallot, and ginger to the pan. Turn over the scallops and sear for 30 seconds more. Pour in the chile-garlic sauce mixture and, once bubbling, add in the cornstarch mixture and the sesame oil. Gently swirl the sauce around the scallops. Turn off the heat and let the mixture simmer and thicken. Season with salt and pepper to taste.

Serve the scallops warm with plenty of sauce. Garnish with the cilantro leaves.

the   een the
the unc   avalanches,
forward in su
thunderous crashings
all combined to give a feeling of unreality and mysterious adventure to our toil.

In appearance we bore no resemblance to the party
who had left civilisation only two months before. Our
faces were burned almost black by the glare of the sun on
the ice-fields, and were seamed and hard from the severity

y
an

hree
e had
to lead
Beyond
d we saw
ead of us
ive miles.
by the huge
either hand.

SAVORY SPICED LENTIL DOUGHNUTS

We serve these unusual doughnuts for appetizers when we wish to have a vegetarian, gluten-free, or vegan option. We learned how to make these from a Southern Indian family that came to stay with us.

MAKES 20 DOUGHNUTS

2 cups skinned black lentils (urad dal), rinsed well

½ cup store-bought or homemade vegetable stock

3 tablespoons nutritional yeast

1 tablespoon grated fresh ginger

1 tablespoon ground cumin

1 tablespoon sea salt, plus more as needed

1 teaspoon minced garlic

1 teaspoon hot pepper sauce

½ teaspoon ground turmeric

½ teaspoon smoked paprika

¼ teaspoon freshly ground black pepper

½ cup sea lettuce or nori sheets, crumbled

½ cup chopped fresh cilantro

2 sprigs curry leaves, minced

Canola oil for frying

Plain yogurt for serving

Rhubarb Chutney (page 291) for serving

In a bowl, soak the lentils in lukewarm water. Cover the bowl with aluminum foil and soak overnight at room temperature.

Drain the lentils and place them in a food processor. Blend the lentils into a fairly smooth paste. Add the stock a tablespoon at a time and process briefly to loosen it up just a touch—you do not want this batter to be too loose. You may not need all of the stock. Add the nutritional yeast, ginger, cumin, salt, garlic, hot pepper sauce, turmeric, paprika, and pepper and process well. Add the sea lettuce, cilantro, and curry leaves and blend until just incorporated but not to the point that the batter turns green. Season with more salt if you like.

Pour the canola oil into a 6-quart heavy casserole or deep-fryer. Warm over medium heat until the oil reaches 365°F on a deep-frying thermometer.

Using clean and oiled hands, drop a heaping tablespoon of batter into the palm of your hand, then place your thumb into the center of the of the batter. Flipping your palm side over on top of your thumb, release the dough so that the dough is now sitting on your thumb. Carefully drop the dough into the hot oil. Repeat with enough dough to fill the casserole but not crowd it. Fry the doughnuts until golden brown, using a large slotted metal spoon to turn them in the hot oil, about 3 minutes. Remove the doughnuts from the oil and drain on paper towels. Season with salt while hot. Repeat to fry the remaining dough in the same manner.

Serve hot with yogurt and rhubarb chutney.

GREEN & RED APPLE CUSTARD TART

When we make apple dishes, we like to mix green apples with red apples for a flavor and texture contrast. This tart is a variation on that theme. We use applesauce (or sometimes apple butter) and a green apple compote with a unique oat crust. A creamy whipped topping brings the flavors together.

MAKES 8 SERVINGS

FOR THE CRUST

Canola oil for greasing

2 cups rolled oats

1 cup all-purpose flour

¼ cup packed light brown sugar

2 teaspoons ground cinnamon

1 teaspoon pure vanilla bean paste or vanilla extract

½ teaspoon sea salt

1 cup unsalted butter, melted

FOR THE RED APPLE FILLING

1¼ cups sweetened condensed milk

1 cup applesauce

½ cup packed light brown sugar

1 large egg

2 teaspoons all-purpose flour

1 teaspoon pure vanilla bean paste or vanilla extract

½ teaspoon sea salt

FOR THE GREEN APPLE COMPOTE

1 green apple, peeled and diced small

1 tablespoon unsalted butter

¼ cup packed light brown sugar

2 tablespoons whiskey

½ teaspoon pure vanilla bean paste or vanilla extract

½ teaspoon sea salt

Cinnamon Whipped Cream (page 288)

To make the crust, grease a 9-inch tart pan with a removable bottom with canola oil. In a bowl, mix together the oats, flour, brown sugar, cinnamon, vanilla, and salt. Pour in the melted butter and mix until the dough comes together. Press the dough into bottom and sides of the prepared pan and refrigerate until ready to use.

To make the red apple filling, preheat the oven to 350°F. In a bowl, whisk together the condensed milk, applesauce, brown sugar, egg, flour, vanilla, and salt and mix until well blended. Pour the mixture into the prepared tart shell.

Bake the tart until the crust is golden and the filling is set, about 35 minutes.

While the tart is baking, make the green apple compote. Place the diced apples into a small sauté pan with the butter, brown sugar, whiskey, vanilla, and salt. Simmer over low heat until the apples are cooked and the sauce has a caramel texture, about 10 minutes. Set aside.

Remove the tart from the oven and let it cool completely on a wire rack.

Prepare the Cinnamon Whipped Cream. To assemble, use a small offset spatula to spread the cooled tart with the green apple compote. Cut into wedges and serve each slice with a dollop of the whipped cream.

FRIED YELLOWEYE ROCKFISH WITH XO SAUCE

At present, rockfish is in abundance and its population is healthy in Alaska, but we always watch for any species that might be stressed by overfishing. Rockfish is lean with a mild flavor that can take on strong seasonings. This recipe shares our love of cooking whole fish. Serve with bowls of sticky rice and soy sauce, for seasoning.

MAKES 2 TO 4 SERVINGS

½ cup cornstarch

Sea salt and freshly ground black pepper

1 whole small rockfish, gutted, scaled, rinsed, and patted dry

1 cup homemade or store-bought XO Sauce (page 294)

Canola oil

In a small bowl, mix the cornstarch, 1 teaspoon salt, and 1 teaspoon pepper.

Place the fish on an 18-by-13-inch baking sheet lined with parchment paper. With a kitchen knife, score the fish diagonally on each side about 3 times. Rub the fish with the XO sauce from head to fin. Rub any remaining sauce in the fish cavity. Let the fish marinate for 30 minutes in the refrigerator.

Remove the fish from the refrigerator and dust it lightly on all sides with the cornstarch mixture.

In a 12-to-14-inch high-sided nonstick sauté pan (depending on the size of your fish), warm 1 inch of oil over medium heat until it reads 350°F on a deep-frying thermometer.

Once the oil is hot, gently ease in the fish. Fry until crisp and golden on one side, about 5 minutes. Then flip the fish over and fry the other side until crisp and golden, about 5 more minutes.

Remove the fish from the oil and place onto a rack to cool. Season with salt. Serve on a platter and share family-style. Pull apart to eat.

ALASKA CRAB TART

In the summer we dress this tart with flowers from the garden. In winter, we use simple herbs with chunks of crabmeat. We serve this at the La Baleine Café as well as at the lodges as part of our breakfast repertoire. Or, sometimes we serve it at lunch with a small bowl of tomato soup. It's lovely at any time of the day.

MAKES 6 TO 12 SERVINGS

FOR THE CUSTARD

4 large eggs

1 cup heavy cream

½ cup sour cream

¼ cup grated Parmigiano-Reggiano cheese

2 tablespoons finely chopped chives

Sea salt and freshly ground black pepper

FOR THE FILLING & TART SHELL

2 ounces uncooked bulk Mexican chorizo sausage

1 medium-size leek, dark green removed, sliced

2 cloves garlic, minced

1 shallot, minced

1 teaspoon fresh thyme leaves

Potato Tart Shell (page 291), baked and cooled

1 cup Alaska king crab meat, picked over for shells

FOR THE HERB & CRAB SALAD

¼ cup fresh cilantro leaves

¼ cup fresh flat-leaf parsley leaves

¼ cup fresh tarragon leaves

½ cup baby arugula

1 tablespoon extra-virgin olive oil

2 teaspoons apple cider vinegar

Sea salt and freshly ground black pepper

1 cup Alaska king crab meat, picked over for shells

Preheat the oven to 325°F.

To make the custard, in a bowl, whisk together the eggs, cream, sour cream, cheese, and chives. Season the mixture lightly with salt and pepper.

To make the filling, brown the chorizo in a sauté pan over medium heat. After 1 minute, add the leek, garlic, shallot, and thyme. Sauté until the leek is tender, about 5 minutes. Season with salt and pepper. Cool the filling.

Arrange the chorizo mixture evenly in the baked and cooled tart shell. Sprinkle in the 1 cup crabmeat. Gently pour in the custard. Bake the tart until the custard is set, about 30 minutes. Remove from the oven and place on a wire rack to cool slightly or completely.

To make the herb and crab salad, in a small bowl, combine the cilantro, parsley, tarragon, and arugula. Dress the greens with the olive oil, cider vinegar, and salt and pepper to taste. Add the remaining 1 cup crab meat and toss lightly.

Top the baked, cooled tart with the herb and crab salad and serve warm or at room temperature, cut into wedges.

ILLUMINATION

As Alaska turns toward the autumnal equinox, days darken and draw in. On some days, we stop whatever we are doing to look skyward to see groups of wild swans gliding overheard in migration to lower latitudes. Those graceful Trumpeter swans flying south are our own elegant harbingers of winter.

Every living thing around us knows winter is on its way. Leaves turn scarlet, fireweed has long faded to puffs of white scattered on the wind, and bright pink rose petals fall to the ground. We start to look up to the peaks surrounding us for "termination dust," that first brush of transitional snow.

Our lives transition along with the seasons. We begin to prepare Tutka Bay Lodge and La Baleine Café for the seven-month winter season as soon as the weather turns colder. We board up windows and doors, we remove liquids that might freeze and burst, and we check for any place where storms could blow their way inside. Foods from the pantry, fridges, and freezers are moved. We donate what is left from the season to those in need. The last act at Tutka Bay is to send our precious fresh spring water gathered all summer back to the sea. It's such hard work to collect water since we are surrounded by saltwater, but returning it feels like a ritual offering.

At Winterlake, we fly in provisions from Anchorage while we can still land floatplanes on the lake. We are not so different than the other animals around us. We bring in planeloads of dog food, stacking big 50-pound sacks ten-high in our storage room. Our sled dogs eat one pound of food per day per dog, and we have twenty dogs. We bring in enough food for us as well, knowing that planes will now be few and far between for the winter months.

The light in the Alaska sky can be captivating in any season, but autumn brings a kind of mysterious sun-shadow contrast that is moody and dramatic. It reminds us to hurry up and harvest the garden and take stock of what we might want to preserve before the first frost. It's a time when the crush of the summer schedule subsides, and we find ourselves with the luxury of time to walk down the Iditarod Trail or explore our old-growth forest path.

A pair of great blue herons returns to Tutka Bay in the fall, their giant slate-gray wings rushing past our field of vision as they croak and swoop from treetop to rock. They are supposed to migrate to South America, we have heard, but these two come back to the tall Sitka spruce

> It's such hard work to collect water since we are surrounded by saltwater, but returning it feels like a ritual offering.

surrounding the lodge each fall and go to some unknown place during the heat of the summer. At Winterlake, we hear the soulful sound of loons crying as they sport their fledgling around the lake, preparing the youngster for their impending departure and journey. If we are lucky, we will see flocks of V-formation Sandhill cranes with their six-foot wingspans flying high overhead from the west, heading south to warmer climes.

It's at this time that we dig out headlamps and lanterns, and we find the stash of candles we will use all winter. We wear our headlamps like indispensable jewels, on our hats or around our necks. We string white lights along railings to brighten our buildings against the dark. We once again marvel at the arctic celestial sky at night without any human light pollution to break the spell.

It has been said that eighty percent of Americans can no longer see stars with any clarity due to city lights. Stargazing becomes our free nighttime entertainment provided by the universe when the sky is clear from clouds or snow. Carl turns off the generator that powers our electricity at Winterlake. He waits until all guests are well asleep, and he turns the diesel-powered generator on again before they wake—but, during that quiet time he listens to the silence, and he reminds us to notice the vast and awe-inspiring skyward wonders that are always in silent motion.

It is a sky theatre of curtains and swirls, arcs, and waves.

In a small window of time at Tutka Bay, our entire cove turns into an ocean wonderland of moving lights as dinoflagellates brighten and swirl in the water. We swirl sticks or paddles into the ocean and watch in amazement as the water lights up. A few brave souls jump into the cold water in a stream of trailing lights like superheroes traveling through a night sky. The official procedure is to take in a deep breath and laugh off the knowledge of how cold the water is, jump in the ocean, then run rapidly into the banya (our wood-fired sauna).

Northern lights begin to reappear. We head outside and turn our attention upward to watch solar ions smash into atoms within Earth's atmosphere. Colors ranging from iridescent green to deep rose and violet mingle and dance together to reveal imagined Gods, fire-bridges to the afterlife, or, as Alaska Inuit believed, the souls of animals they hunted. We believe the northern lights rain special energy over our lake and our house, and over the sled dogs sleeping quietly in their dog lot.

Autumn is the time of year when we are in and out of the kitchen, running to the garden or greenhouse for a last-gathered bunch of flat-leaf parsley or a handful of lemon verbena, clipping and stringing lemon thyme and mint along the ledges in the bar and wellness room to dry for winter use. We pick and pickle blueberries and cherries, we freeze black and red currants to bring out in the dead of winter. In some years, we hang our still-green tomatoes upside down in the greenhouse to continue to ripen and eat at just the right time. We harvest potatoes, carrots, and parsnips for winter cold storage, and we make sure our freezers are filled with reindeer, red salmon, king salmon, and crab.

Before the ice freezes, at Tutka Bay, Gus pulls off the dock and heads to Homer with a boat full of departing employees chatting and joking. At Winterlake, a final floatplane lifts off the lake, with the loons punctuating the quiet with their haunting call as a kind of farewell. It's the time of year we say goodbye to our summer employees. Fond farewells and hugs, exchanges of addresses and promises to keep in touch, end-of-season music and bonfires by the water, are all sweet and sad at the same moment. A few employees stay on through the winter months, but most head out to new adventures, warmer shores, jobs half-way around the globe. We are all a well-traveled bunch, and all of us agree on one thing—that our two lodges are located in one of the most beautiful places on the planet.

When summer guests and staff have all gone, we sit in the living room of the lodge near the woodstove. We revel in the hard work we accomplished during the summer months, the guests we met, the new friends we worked with, and the stories we heard and told.

BLACK GARLIC YOLK & HONEY PASTA

This beautiful pasta is inspired by our farmer friend Lori, who makes black garlic and has honeybees. It is our take on pasta carbonara. Black garlic is available in Asian markets. It's deliciously sweet and dark.

MAKES 4 TO 6 SERVINGS

6 large, fresh egg yolks

2 tablespoons heavy cream

2 cups unsalted butter

2 cloves black garlic, thinly sliced

1 tablespoon honey

1 pound dried tagliatelle (or other) pasta

Sea salt and freshly ground black pepper

½ cup coarsely chopped Rhubarb Salmon Bacon (page 40)

1 cup freshly grated Parmigiano-Reggiano cheese

Shaved Parmigiano-Reggiano cheese for serving

In a bowl, whisk the egg yolks well. Add the cream and whisk together. Set aside.

In a small saucepan over low heat, combine the butter and garlic, stirring once. Let the butter simmer until the milk solids separate from the clear butterfat, about 5 minutes. Remove the garlic butter from the heat and let stand for 5 minutes. Then, using a large metal spoon, skim off and discard the foamy milk proteins that have risen to the top. Ladle the clear, yellow clarified garlic butter into a small bowl, discarding any remaining milk solids in the saucepan. Stir in the honey.

While whisking the egg yolks, add the warm butter mixture a tablespoon at a time. When you've added about half of the butter, pour in the rest of the butter, whisking until smooth. This process of adding the warm butter slowly to the eggs helps prevent the egg yolks from cooking. Set aside.

Cook the pasta in boiling salted water until al dente, about 12 minutes. Drain the pasta and put it back into the pot.

Add the salmon bacon and Parmigiano-Reggiano to the pot with the pasta and toss well.

Once the pasta has cooled slightly, pour in the egg yolk-cream-butter mixture, coating the pasta. Finish with some black pepper and shaved Parmigiano-Reggiano.

BLACK COD KAMAMESHI

When sake, miso, and black are cod combined, you know it is going to be good. Serve with pickled vegetables or Kelp Pickles (page 290). Shiitake mushrooms have a rich, buttery, savory flavor that complements this. Is it an Alaska dish? Combined with our black cod and Japan's flavor palate, it's a marriage made on the Pacific Rim.

MAKES 6 SERVINGS

FOR THE MARINATED FISH

¼ cup sake

¼ cup mirin

4 tablespoons white miso paste

3 tablespoons sugar

4 black cod fillets,
    about ½ pound each

FOR THE RICE

4 cups short-grain sushi rice

4 cups store-bought or
    homemade chicken stock

¼ cup diced yellow onion

1-inch piece kombu seaweed

4 cloves garlic, sliced

¼ pound shiitake mushrooms,
    stemmed and torn into
    bitesize pieces

FOR THE SAUCE

4 tablespoons soy sauce

2 tablespoons honey

2 tablespoon sake

1 tablespoon mirin

1 teaspoon toasted sesame oil

4 green onions, thinly sliced

1 leek, light part only, washed
    and thinly sliced

2 large eggs, whisked

¼ cup enoki mushrooms

Two days before you plan to serve this dish, bring the sake and mirin to a boil in a saucepan for 20 seconds. Reduce the heat to low and whisk in the miso until smooth. Increase the heat to high and add the sugar, whisking constantly until dissolved. Let cool to room temperature. Pat the cod fillets thoroughly dry. Slather the miso marinade over the fish and place in a bowl. Cover the bowl tightly with Bee's Wrap and marinate in the refrigerator for 2 days.

To make the rice, put the rice in a bowl and cover with cold water. Swirl the rice grains around with your fingers to release any starch. Pour through a strainer. Repeat the process three more times, or until the water runs clear. Place the rice and the stock in a large pot over medium heat. Add the onion, kombu, garlic, and mushrooms. Cover the pot and cook over medium-low heat until the broth is absorbed, 15 to 20 minutes total.

While the rice is cooking, heat a sauté pan over high heat. Lightly wipe off any excess marinade on the fillets, but do not rinse. Place the fish skin-side-up in the pan and cook until the bottom browns, about 3 minutes. Gently turn over the fish and cook until the other side is browned, 2 to 3 minutes. Transfer to a plate.

To make the sauce, in a small bowl, stir together the soy sauce, honey, sake, mirin, and sesame oil and set aside.

When the rice is about halfway done, uncover the pot and lay the seared fish, green onions, and leek on top of the rice. Pour in the sauce and beaten eggs. Top with the enoki mushrooms. Cover the pot and continue cooking until the rice is tender and the liquid has been absorbed.

APPLE CIDER MARSHMALLOWS

Imagine we are deep in autumn in Alaska and we are sitting together by the water. The trees are losing their leaves, the sun is lying low, and we are at the bonfire. You skewer the marshmallow onto a stick and place it into the fire. When perfectly charred, you dunk the marshmallow into your hot cider or sandwich it between slices of green apple. These marshmallows set the perfect tone for a lovely fall gathering.

MAKES 16

2 cups apple cider

Canola oil for greasing

½ cup powdered sugar

½ cup cornstarch

3 (¼-ounce) packages powdered unflavored gelatin

½ teaspoon ground cinnamon

¼ teaspoon ground cardamom

¼ teaspoon ground nutmeg

1 teaspoon pure vanilla bean paste or vanilla extract

½ cup granulated sugar

½ cup packed light brown sugar

½ cup birch or other syrup

½ cup honey

½ teaspoon sea salt

2 egg whites

In a small saucepan, simmer the apple cider over medium-high heat until reduced by half, about 10 minutes. Let cool slightly.

In a bowl, mix together the powdered sugar and cornstarch. Line a 9-by-9-inch baking pan with greased parchment paper. Then, lightly dust the parchment with some of the powdered sugar-cornstarch mixture, being sure to get the sides, too.

Pour the cooled cider into the bowl of a stand mixer fitted with the whisk attachment. Stir in the gelatin, cinnamon, cardamom, nutmeg, and vanilla.

In a small saucepan over medium heat, stir together both sugars, birch syrup, honey, and salt. Attach a candy thermometer to the side of the pan and submerge it in the mixture. Boil the mixture until syrupy and the thermometer reads 240°F.

Add the 2 egg whites to the mixer with the cider-spice mixture. Whisk on medium speed until the egg whites form medium-stiff peaks, about 5 minutes. Turn the mixer to low speed. While mixing, slowly and carefully pour the hot syrup down the inside of the bowl. Increase the mixer speed to high and beat until a whipped, fluffy, opaque batter forms, about 5 minutes. Gently pour the batter into the prepared pan, spreading evenly with a rubber spatula. Lightly dust some of the powdered sugar-cornstarch mixture on the top. Set the marshmallow aside for 30 minutes to firm up.

Remove the marshmallow square from the pan. With a large, sharp knife, cut the marshmallow into 16 squares. Lightly dust each square with some of the powdered sugar-cornstarch mixture. Place the squares into an airtight container. Marshmallows will keep for 4–6 days.

FERMENTED HONEY CARROT CAKES

Alaska has some of the best honey in the world. And Alaska carrots are the sweetest. Both being harvested in the fall, carrots and honey are used in many ways this time of year. To play around with flavors, we use fermented honey's lemony, sweet tang to offset the carrots. Use any leftover crumble on cereal or other baked goods.

MAKES 12 SERVINGS

FOR THE CARROT CAKES

2 cups unsalted butter,
    at room temperature

1 cup granulated sugar

½ cup packed light brown sugar

6 tablespoons Fermented Honey
    (page 290)

4 eggs

2 teaspoon pure vanilla bean paste
    or vanilla extract

4 cups all-purpose flour

2 teaspoons baking powder

½ teaspoon baking soda

2 teaspoons sea salt

1 teaspoon ground cinnamon

¼ teaspoon ground nutmeg

1½ cups sour cream

2 cups freshly grated carrots

FOR THE CRUMBLE TOPPING

3 cups all-purpose flour

1 cup packed light brown sugar

1 tablespoon sea salt

1 cup unsalted butter, melted

To make the cakes, in a stand mixer fitted with the paddle attachment, combine the butter, both sugars, and honey. Beat on medium speed until light and fluffy, about 2 minutes. Reduce the mixer speed to low and add the eggs one at a time until well incorporated. Mix in the vanilla. Scrape down the bowl well.

In a small bowl, mix together the flour, baking powder, baking soda, salt, cinnamon, and nutmeg. While beating on low speed, add the flour mixture to the bowl and mix until just combined. Stop the mixer and scrape down the bowl. On low speed, add the sour cream and grated carrots and mix just until incorporated. Take care not to overmix. Refrigerate for 20 minutes.

Preheat the oven to 325°F and grease two 8½-by-4½-inch loaf pans. Line a baking sheet with parchment paper.

Transfer the batter to the prepared pans, dividing evenly. Bake the cakes for about 20 minutes. The cakes will not be fully baked at this point.

To make the topping, in a bowl, mix the flour, brown sugar, and salt. Add the butter and mix with a wooden spoon. Spread the mixture evenly in the prepared baking sheet. Bake until light golden brown, rotating the pan halfway through, about 10 minutes.

Sprinkle some of the baked crumble over the top of each partially baked cake. You will have some crumble left over. Rotate the cakes and continue baking until a cake tester inserted into the center of the cakes comes out clean, 15 to 20 minutes.

Let the cakes cool completely before removing them from the pan. Cut into slices to serve.

BLUEBERRY CURD SANDWICH COOKIES

Blueberries are abundant in Alaska cuisine, both in winter and in summer. This is a lovely way to remember those summer days when blueberries were still on the bush. Luckily for us, blueberries are incredibly healthy, so you can feel okay about indulging in these sweet treats.

MAKES 48 COOKIE SANDWICHES

1 cup unsalted butter, at room temperature

4 ounces cream cheese, at room temperature

1 cup sugar

1 large egg yolk

1 teaspoon pure vanilla bean paste
   or vanilla extract

1 teaspoon finely grated lemon zest

2½ cups all-purpose flour

1 tablespoon fresh lemon thyme leaves

¼ teaspoon sea salt

Blueberry Curd (page 287)

Place the butter, cream cheese, and sugar in the bowl of a stand mixer fitted with the paddle attachment. Beat on medium speed until light and fluffy, about 2 minutes. Add the egg yolk, vanilla, and lemon zest and mix well. Reduce the mixer speed to medium and mix in the flour, thyme, and salt just until combined and a dough forms.

Divide the dough into 2 equal pieces. Place each piece on a lightly floured work surface and shape it into a roll about 12 inches long. Wrap each roll in clean kitchen towels and chill for 20 minutes.

Preheat the oven to 350°F. Have ready 4 nonstick 13-by-18-inch baking sheets (or use 2 baking sheets in batches).

Remove the dough logs from the refrigerator and cut each log into ¼-inch slices. Place the slices onto the baking sheets, placing 24 cookies on each pan and spacing them 1 inch apart. Bake until the tops are no longer moist, about 10 minutes. Let the cookies cool completely before filling.

Transfer the blueberry curd to 2 piping bags fitted with medium round tips. Pipe the curd onto the flat side of one cookie, starting with an outer ring and working inward. Place another cookie on top, flat-side in, and press gently to adhere the two cookies together with the curd. Repeat with the remaining cookies and blueberry curd. Serve right away.

RED BEET & BARLEY SCONES

We know these might sound a little heavy, but think of yourself in a log cabin, deep in winter. You've just started the woodstove fire, so it is still a little dark and very cold. Wouldn't you love to sit down to these warm and savory scones with a hot pot of coffee, a good book to read, and the whole day ahead of you?

MAKES 6 SCONES

Canola oil for greasing, optional

1½ cups all-purpose flour

¾ cup barley flour, plus extra for dusting

2 tablespoons packed light brown sugar

1 tablespoon baking powder

1 teaspoon sea salt

½ cup chilled unsalted butter, cut into pieces

1 cup plain yogurt

¼ cup buttermilk

1 teaspoon apple cider vinegar

1 red beet, peeled

Berry jam and butter for serving

Preheat the oven to 350°F. Grease a baking sheet or line with parchment paper.

In a stand mixer fitted with the paddle attachment, mix together both flours, the brown sugar, baking powder, and salt. Add the butter and mix on low speed until the butter forms pea-sized pieces in the flour mixture. Add the yogurt, buttermilk, and vinegar and mix just until the mixture forms a sticky dough. Using a box grater, shred the beets and gently fold them and any beet juice into the dough.

Dust a work surface with some of the barley flour. Pat the dough into a circle about 9 inches in diameter and 1 inch thick. Using a large chef knife, cut the dough into 6 equal wedges. Transfer the dough wedges to the prepared baking sheet. Place on the center oven rack and bake until the scones are golden brown and firm, 15 to 20 minutes.

Serve warm with berry jam and butter.

PARSNIP CAKE WITH APPLE CIDER CREAM

Kirsten was skeptical about this cake when Mandy introduced it, but now she is a fan. It's beautiful to look at, aromatic, and not too sweet. Mandy bakes with vanilla paste, which can be a little expensive. Measure for measure, it's the same as vanilla extract (just don't use imitation vanilla extract!). Substitute a little bit of pureed dates if you don't have vanilla.

MAKES 8 SERVINGS

Butter, for greasing

FOR THE CAKE
1¼ cups all-purpose flour
2 teaspoons ground cinnamon
1 teaspoon ground ginger
2 teaspoons baking powder
½ cup canola oil
½ cup whole milk

2 teaspoons pure vanilla bean paste or vanilla extract
3 large eggs
1 cup sugar
2 cups shredded parsnips
½ cup walnut pieces

FOR THE APPLE CIDER CREAM
8 ounces cream cheese, at room temperature

1 cup packed light brown sugar
1 cup heavy cream
1 teaspoon pure vanilla bean paste or vanilla extract
1 tablespoon ground cinnamon
2 tablespoons apple cider
¼ cup walnuts, for grating

Preheat the oven to 350°F. Line a 9-inch round cake pan with parchment paper and butter the bottom and sides well.

To make the cake, in a bowl, mix together the flour, cinnamon, ginger, and baking powder. In a separate small bowl, mix together the oil, milk, and vanilla.

In the bowl of a stand mixer fitted with the whisk attachment, whip the eggs and sugar on medium speed until the mixture is pale in color and when you lift the whisk the batter falls slowly in a ribbon that holds its shape, about 5 minutes. On the lowest mixer speed, mix in half of the flour mixture alternating with half of the milk mixture. Stir until just combined. Fold in the parsnips and walnuts.

Pour the batter into the prepared pan and bake until golden brown on top and a cake tester inserted into the center comes out clean, 15 to 20 minutes. Let cool completely in the pan.

To make the apple cider cream, in the bowl of a stand mixer fitted with the whisk attachment, beat the cream cheese and brown sugar on medium speed until incorporated. Drizzle in the cream and beat just until the mixture is fluffy and smooth, about 5 minutes. Add the vanilla, cinnamon, and cider and whisk until blended, about 20 seconds. Set aside at room temperature.

Remove the cake from the pan and place it on a plate. Generously frost the top of the cake. Using a cheese grater, grate the walnuts over the top. Cut the cake into wedges to serve.

SOURDOUGH APPLE FRITTERS

Sourdough is an Alaska kitchen staple, but if you don't have a starter going, substitute ½ cup bread flour mixed with ½ cup water for the starter. We like Granny Smith apples as they hold up well to Alaska conditions.

MAKES ABOUT 12 FRITTERS, DEPENDING ON APPLE SIZE

1½ cups sugar

½ teaspoon sea salt

2 teaspoons ground cinnamon

1 cup sourdough starter

1 teaspoon baking soda

¼ teaspoon ground cardamom

Canola oil for frying

2 Granny Smith apples, peeled, cored, and diced

In a small bowl, mix together ½ cup of the sugar, the salt, and 1 teaspoon of the cinnamon and set aside.

In a bowl, whisk together the sourdough starter, baking soda, the remaining 1 cup sugar, the cardamom, and remaining 1 teaspoon cinnamon until blended.

Pour 2 inches of oil into a 4 quart casserole and place over medium heat. Warm until the oil reaches 365°F on a deep-frying thermometer.

While the oil is heating, add the apples to the sourdough batter and gently coat all sides. With a small cookie scoop, scoop a portion of the apple-sourdough mixture and gently drop it into the oil. Let the apples bubble and float in the oil until all sides are golden brown, about 2 minutes. Use a slotted spoon to remove the fritters and lightly tap on the edge of the pot to drain the excess oil. Transfer the fritters directly to the bowl with the cinnamon-sugar mixture and coat all sides. Set the fritters aside on paper towels and cover with a clean kitchen towel to keep warm. Repeat the process with the remaining apple-sourdough mixture.

Serve warm.

ROOT CELLAR RABBIT STEW

We can access rabbits for eating pretty easily here in Alaska. If you can't find rabbit meat in a regular grocery store, try your local butcher. Some butchers sell half-a-rabbit packages, which would be fine in this recipe. We serve this over hot buttered basmati rice.

MAKES 4 SERVINGS

6 strips bacon, diced

4 rabbit legs (about 2½ pounds)

Sea salt and freshly ground black pepper

4 tablespoons all-purpose flour

4 tablespoons canola oil

2 yellow onions, halved, then sliced ¼ inch thick

6 cloves garlic, thinly sliced

2 tablespoons tomato paste

4 small yellow potatoes, diced

2 carrots, peeled and diced

2 small golden beets, peeled and diced

1 parsnip, peeled and diced

1 turnip, peeled and diced

1 cup mixed wild mushrooms, cleaned and torn into bite-size pieces

2 (14-ounce) cans chopped tomatoes

1 cup dry sherry or white wine

4 cups store-bought or homemade chicken stock

1 sprig fresh rosemary

1 large sprig fresh thyme

2 bay leaves

2 cups shelled fresh or thawed frozen peas

Hot cooked rice or noodles for serving

In a 6-quart casserole over medium-low heat, cook the diced bacon until the fat has rendered and the meat is crisp, about 2 minutes. Using a slotted spoon, transfer the bacon to a plate, leaving the fat in the pan.

Lightly season the rabbit with salt and pepper and sprinkle with the flour, tossing to coat evenly. Warm the pan with the bacon fat over medium heat. Add the rabbit legs and cook until brown, about 5 minutes on each side. Use tongs to transfer the browned legs to a metal rack set over a baking sheet and set aside.

Add the oil to the same casserole. Add the onions and garlic, and sauté over medium heat until tender, about 7 minutes. Add the tomato paste, potatoes, carrots, beets, parsnip, turnip, and mushrooms and sauté until lightly caramelized, about 3 minutes. Lay the rabbit pieces on top of the vegetables and add the tomatoes, sherry, and stock. The ingredients should be submerged in liquid; if they are not, add water to supplement. Add the rosemary, thyme, and bay leaves. Bring the liquid to a low boil, then reduce the heat and simmer until the rabbit is tender and flakes off the bone, about 1 hour or longer, depending on the tenderness of the meat.

Remove the rabbit from the stew and pick the meat off the bones. Return the meat to the stew and heat through. (Save the bones to make stock, if you like.) Stir in the peas and reserved bacon and season to taste with salt and pepper.

To serve, divide the rice or noodles among 4 serving bowls and ladle the stew over the top.

STALKS & STEMS SAUCE

This sauce evolved out of our no-waste policy in our kitchens. It's easy to make and vary in your own kitchen: just save the stalks and any bits of leaves from the greens you clean. This makes a lovely sauce for pasta or you can use it as a salad dressing.

MAKES ABOUT 4 CUPS

4 cups water

2 cups chopped cauliflower stalks (1-inch pieces)

2 cups chopped broccoli stalks (1-inch pieces)

2 cups chopped spinach stems (1-inch pieces)

1½ cups chopped kale stems (1-inch pieces)

1 cup chopped fresh parsley stems (1-inch pieces)

1 cup raw unsalted cashews

½ cup nutritional yeast

1 tablespoon granulated garlic

1 teaspoon hot pepper sauce

Juice of ½ lemon

1 teaspoon sea salt, or more to taste

In a saucepan, bring the water to a boil over medium-high heat. Add the cauliflower and broccoli stalks, and the spinach, kale, and parsley stems and simmer until the thickest stalks are tender, about 5 minutes.

Transfer the contents of the pan, including the liquid, to a blender and blend until smooth. Add the cashews and nutritional yeast and continue to blend until smooth. Add the garlic, hot pepper sauce, lemon, and salt and blend briefly.

The sauce can be served warm or cold. It will keep in the refrigerator for 1 week.

BARLEY CONGEE WITH DUCK & SEAWEED

We learned how to make rice congee from our frequent Chinese guests. Here's Mandy's version of a barley congee with duck confit, an interesting variation that is warming on a cold morning. We serve small bowls of congee within a lavish table spread of breads, eggs, and meats.

MAKES 6 SERVINGS

1 cup pearl barley

1 tablespoon canola oil

1 yellow onion, diced

½ pound domestic mushrooms, roughly chopped

3 cloves garlic, minced

½ teaspoon sea salt

12 cups store-bought or homemade chicken stock

1 tablespoon soy sauce

2 teaspoons Thai fish sauce (nam pla)

1 pound Duck Confit, flaked (page 288)

4 to 6 inches sea lettuce or nori

Red pepper flakes for garnish

Rinse the barley under cold water. Dry the barley well on a few layers of paper towels.

In a large 6-quart casserole over low heat, stir together the oil and barley. Cook the barley until you detect a toasty, popcorn-y aroma, about 5 minutes. Add the onion, mushrooms, garlic, and salt. Sauté, stirring constantly, for 2 minutes.

Add 6 cups of the chicken stock, cover the casserole, and simmer the soup for 2 hours. Every 10 minutes or so, insert a whisk into the soup and carefully break down the barley a bit each time. After 2 hours, the barley should expand and become mushy.

Add the remaining 6 cups of stock to the pot. The consistency should be that of loose porridge. Stir in the soy sauce, fish sauce, and duck meat. Top with the crumbled sea lettuce.

To serve, ladle the congee into bowls, dividing evenly, and garnish with the pepper flakes. Serve warm.

SOUR RED CABBAGE & BEET SOUP

This is a favorite autumn soup that is beautiful in color. We think that it matches our Alaskan skies, trees, and even the moody water as we begin the transition from summer to winter. We love oxtails in soup, and they add a particular sheen and gelatinous texture to this version of a Russian borscht. Ask for oxtails at your local butcher.

MAKES 4 SERVINGS

4 red beets

Canola oil

Sea salt and freshly ground black pepper

1 pound oxtails

6 small red potatoes, quartered

1 large carrot, peeled and diced

2 cloves garlic, thinly sliced

½ red onion, diced

1 pound roma tomatoes, peeled and diced

¼ pound domestic mushrooms, stemmed

½ small head red cabbage, shredded

6 cups store-bought or homemade beef stock

¼ cup fresh lemon juice

5 pitted prunes, diced

½ cup sour cream

Preheat the oven to 375°F.

Rub the beets in oil and then season lightly with salt and pepper. Wrap the beets individually with aluminum foil and bake until they are soft and the skin comes away easily, about 1 hour. Remove from the oven and set aside to cool.

Season the oxtails on all sides with salt and pepper. In a 6-quart casserole over high heat, warm 3 tablespoons canola oil. Add the oxtails and sear until browned, about 5 minutes on each side. Remove the oxtails from the pan and set aside. Heat 2 more tablespoons of oil in the same pot. Add the potatoes, carrot, garlic, onion, tomatoes, and mushrooms. Cook the vegetables over medium heat, stirring occasionally, until they begin to soften, about 5 minutes. Add the cabbage and the oxtails to the pot. Pour in the beef stock. Turn up the heat to medium-high, bring the liquid just to a boil, then immediately turn down the heat so that the liquid just simmers. Simmer the soup until the oxtail meat falls off the bones, 2½ to 3 hours.

Remove the meat from the oxtail bones and flake the meat with a fork. Add the meat back to the soup. Discard the bones.

Peel the beets and dice them. In a small bowl, combine the beets and lemon juice and toss well. Add the beets and juice to the soup along with the prunes. Simmer the soup for about 10 minutes to heat through. Stir in the sour cream and season to taste with salt and pepper.

Ladle the soup into bowls and serve hot.

SNOW DAY

The morning starts with just a hint of winter garnet and graphite washing over the mountains across the lake. The sky will flood to scarlet soon, and the dawn chorus of black-capped chickadees will announce Mandy's presence as she walks from her cabin to the kitchen, boots crunching over dry snow. She stops and looks at the ancient birch tree draped in white and breathes in the last moments of quiet on this, the busiest day of the year. It's the Iditarod. Mandy knows this will be a hard workday. But she has no idea what's already set in motion, heading her way.

In the kitchen, lanterns glow along the long homemade table piled with fur hats, heavy winter jackets, mittens as big as pie plates, and thick Nalgene water bottles covered in duct tape. The first musher arrived at 4:00 in the morning, a tiny bobbing headlamp beam from across the lake, growing bigger until the sled dogs in our lot acknowledged the presence of strange dogs and began to howl. The tent camp of checkers and veterinarians scurried over the ice, slashes of headlamp lights darting here and there against the dark sky, preparing for the incoming team.

Iditarod day, in one moment, is exhilarating, with palpable energy on the lake. At the same moment, it is disruptive to our own sense of isolation and serenity. As airplanes land and disgorge people in the bright winter sun and more dog teams arrive, there's a feeling that something is happening, a moment in time to remember, a memorable grand adventure we are witness to. Yet, the smooth perfect snow on our lake becomes a marred imprint of the day's chaos—dog prints, people prints, airplane tracks, and snow machine marks. Thankfully, all will be erased with the next healing snowfall, and soon, the traveling carnival of people, dogs, and planes will move west along the trail to leave us again with our dawn chorus and quietude.

Mandy makes "musher meals," a tradition we started many years ago. We feed any musher who wishes to walk the small incline trail from the lake into our kitchen. Some years, it is black beans simmered in chicken stock and garlic with orange juice, tomatoes, and cumin and fragrant rice. This year, the base is steamed barley with winter vegetables from the root cellar. Fried eggs and a scoop of freshly made salsa go onto the barley. The kitchen team makes 25 gallons of chopped tomatoes, red onions, limes, and cilantro before every Iditarod. It's a luxury we have such a thing as fresh salsa so far away from any city or store.

> Iditarod day, in one moment, is exhilarating, with palpable energy on the lake.

The busy morning moves into an equally busy afternoon, and the light on the lake starts to change. Mushers begin to slow down to a few weary, red-eyed stragglers who perhaps won't see the wooden arches of Nome this time. The leaders are long down the trail moving past Rainy Pass and onto Rohn and Nikolai, and the race surges up the trail.

Mandy finds a quiet moment, and she removes her apron for a quick walk along the lake before she starts dinner for the overnight lodge guests. Dog straw blows over the snow as the sky deepens and darkens. Mandy feels there is something not quite right about the scene. There are still too many people on the lake, tourists dropped off by air taxis earlier in the day to experience a race "checkpoint," dressed in their windbreakers and sneakers.

Gunmetal clouds heavy with snow move in from the east and quickly descend over the lake. The few pilots remaining look up to the sky, gather their passengers, and leave. The remaining tourists have no idea of the significance of the weather change and what it might mean for them. They stumble along the ice, taking pictures, laughing with each other. Mandy knows, and as she turns back toward the lodge, she wonders how long the impending snowstorm might last.

Inside the kitchen, where the only lodge telephone is located, there is momentary pandemonium. A flood of calls from pilots say they can't pick up their passengers they had dropped off in the morning. There isn't enough daylight now to fly, and the visibility is poor. Snow is falling in giant flakes over anyone standing on the lake. And, there are thirty tourists standing outside our kitchen door.

Gunmetal clouds heavy with snow move in from the east and quickly descend over the lake.

The Iditarod Sled Dog Race commemorates an event in Alaska's history when people came together to help other people isolated from the world and in need. Then, it was for a vaccine to tamper a flu epidemic, and now, at the kitchen door, it is for food and shelter and warmth. The wellness room, a quiet sanctuary in the lodge for meditation and yoga, is quickly turned into a refuge center for the stranded tourists. Carl pulls a table into the middle of the room and sets up a drink station with fresh water from our well. Mandy makes beans and rice, chicken, and fresh cumin tortillas for the stranded tourists' dinner.

One day turns into two turns into three and then four. Snow falls, and the lodge team works with urgency to rake the heavy snow off of cabin roofs, so they won't collapse. Each day, the tourists reveal their personalities and individuality more. Adventurous irritation turns to impatience, to despair, then resolution. A young couple meet, and later in life, they will marry, bonded by the experience of their Alaska adventure. The snow is so deep, older people use Carl's ski poles to navigate the path to the outhouse.

And, Mandy keeps cooking. She makes stews and soups and cornbread from the stored cornmeal. She uses up all the lentils and rice, the black beans, and navy beans, the dried fruits, and the dried mushrooms. Mandy spaces out moments of surprise, like the last of a fresh salad and a big cake for dessert to keep spirits up. The lodge crew needs fuel for the hard work and long days of shoveling snow. The kitchen is the engine that keeps everyone alive.

Finally, skies clear, and birds dart between branches of the spruce and birch. Sun spreads over the lake, softening the lines of the trees with branches bending with heavy snow. Carl and crew work on putting in a runway with snow machines, tamping down the snow over and again until it is firm enough to support an airplane. They line the runway with fresh spruce branches to outline it clearly from overhead. Tourists begin to fold up their sleeping bags and wander outside. Soon, the drone of airplanes can be heard.

Snow days teach us to be self-sufficient. In Alaska, food security is an important issue. Canning and preserving and foraging are not merely popular cultural hobbies. They are life-saving survival strategies.

Kirsten cleans up the wellness room and puts on some wintery music. Mandy surveys her depleted pantry shelves and plans for restocking. She makes a cobbled-together dinner to celebrate our own survival. We gather at the table, staff diving into a mushroom stew made with bits of this and that. We take a deep sigh and laugh at all we've seen over the past few days. Outside, it begins to snow again. The lake is perfectly smooth, without a trace of anyone.

WHITE RUSSIAN COFFEE CAKE

We occasionally make our own liqueurs for the holiday season, but we almost always have coffee liqueur in the pantry to bake with. This is a favorite during the frequent coffee breaks the crew takes to warm up on cold winter days.

MAKES ABOUT 12 SERVINGS

Canola oil for greasing

FOR THE FILLING

1 cup pecans, toasted and chopped

½ cup packed light brown sugar

2 tablespoons coffee liqueur

1 tablespoon unsweetened cocoa powder

1 teaspoon ground cinnamon

FOR THE CAKE

2¾ cups all-purpose flour

1½ teaspoons baking powder

1 teaspoon sea salt

¾ cup heavy cream

¼ cup coffee liqueur

1 cup unsalted butter, at room temperature

1½ cups granulated sugar

4 eggs

2 teaspoons pure vanilla bean paste or vanilla extract

FOR THE GLAZE

1 cup powdered sugar, sifted

2 tablespoons coffee liqueur

2 tablespoons heavy cream

Preheat the oven to 325°F. Grease a standard-size fluted Bundt pan and set aside.

To make the filling, in a bowl, mix together the pecans, brown sugar, coffee liqueur, cocoa powder, and cinnamon. Set aside.

To make the cake, in a bowl, whisk together the flour, baking powder, and salt. Set aside. In a small bowl, whisk together the heavy cream and coffee liqueur. Set aside.

In a stand mixer fitted with the whisk attachment, cream together the butter and sugar until light and fluffy, about 2 minutes. Beat in the eggs one at a time. Add the vanilla and mix well. Scrape down the sides of the bowl. Add the flour mixture 1 cup at a time alternately with the cream-coffee liqueur mixture in ½ cup additions, mixing well each time. Pour half of the batter into the prepared Bundt pan. Sprinkle the filling mixture evenly onto the batter, then pour the rest of the batter over the top. Bake until the cake is firm to touch in the center of one side and a cake tester comes out clean, about 1 hour.

While the cake is baking, make the glaze. In a bowl, whisk together the powdered sugar, coffee liqueur, and heavy cream until smooth. Set the glaze aside.

Let the cake cool for 10 minutes in the pan, then invert the pan onto a wire rack and remove the pan. Once the cake is at room temperature, drizzle the glaze over the cake.

To serve, slice the cake along the Bundt ridges.

BARLEY BOWL MUSHER MEAL

Our musher meals are filling on a cold winter day. This version has duck confit, egg, and a delicious black garlic dressing. It's something a musher could only dream about as they make their way via dogsled to Winterlake Lodge.

MAKES 2 SERVINGS

FOR THE DRESSING

6 cloves black garlic

1 clove fresh garlic, sliced

1 small shallot, sliced

4 tablespoons apple cider vinegar

1 teaspoon yellow miso

½ tablespoon honey

6 tablespoons canola oil, plus more as needed

Sea salt and freshly ground black pepper

FOR THE BARLEY

1 cup pearl barley, rinsed well

3 cups store-bought or homemade chicken stock

Sea salt and freshly ground black pepper

½ cup fresh flat leaf parsley leaves

2 tablespoons unsalted butter

1 teaspoon minced garlic

FOR THE HONEY-ROASTED VEGETABLES

1 small butternut squash, peeled and cut into 1-inch chunks

2 red or yellow beets, peeled and diced

¼ cup Fermented Honey (page 290)

⅓ cup extra-virgin olive oil

Sea salt and freshly ground black pepper

1 cup Duck Confit (page 288)

2 fried eggs, over-medium

To make the dressing, in a blender, blend the black garlic, fresh garlic, and shallot. Add the vinegar, miso, and honey. While the blender is running, add the oil in a steady stream to emulsify. Season with salt and pepper to taste. Set aside.

To make the barley, combine the barley and stock in a saucepan with a teaspoon of salt and bring to a boil over high heat. Reduce the heat until the liquid just simmers. Cover and cook, stirring occasionally, until the barley is tender, 25 to 30 minutes. Discard any extra liquid left in the pan. Add the parsley, butter, and garlic and mix, fluffing the barley grains with a fork. Season to taste with salt and pepper. Keep the barley mixture warm.

Preheat the oven to 425°F. Line a rimmed baking sheet with aluminum foil.

To make the vegetables, place the diced squash on half of the lined pan. Place the beets on the other half of pan. Mix together the honey and olive oil, then pour it over the squash and beets, dividing evenly. Season with salt and pepper. Toss the vegetables lightly in the honey-oil mixture. Roast the vegetables in the oven until the beets and squash are tender, about 20 minutes.

To assemble the dish, divide the warm barley mixture among 2 bowls. Divide the warm squash and beets between the bowls, then add the duck confit, dividing evenly. Drizzle the ingredients with the dressing. Top each bowl with an egg. Serve warm.

SPICY RICE DUMPLINGS WITH SMOKED SALMON

There is a large Korean influence on the food culture in Alaska, and we can get good Korean food right here—particularly in Anchorage. This is a Korean-influenced dish that is popular with our staff and our young grandson. It's good with cheddar cheese instead of mozzarella, if you prefer. We don't serve it to our guests at the lodges yet, but it is a special at the café served with halibut and ramen noodles.

MAKES 4 TO 6 SERVINGS

3 cups rice flour

1 teaspoon sea salt

2 cups water

3 teaspoons toasted sesame oil

½ cup flaked hot-smoked (kippered) salmon

Canola oil

½ yellow onion, sliced

2 cups chopped green cabbage

2 cloves garlic, minced

¼ cup Korean chile paste

1 tablespoon soy sauce

3 tablespoons sugar

2 cups store-bought or homemade chicken stock

1-inch piece kombu seaweed

1 tablespoon sesame seeds

2 green onions, thinly sliced

1 cup shredded whole-milk mozzarella cheese

In a bowl, mix together the rice flour and salt. Stirring with a fork, pour in the water. Stir the mixture until a rough dough forms. Place the dough onto a piece of moistened cheesecloth and place in a steamer set over low heat. Steam the dough until it has a texture resembling modeling clay, about 20 minutes.

Transfer the steamed rice flour dough to the bowl of a stand mixer fitted with the paddle attachment. Add 1 teaspoon of the sesame oil and the salmon. Mix on low speed until the dough comes together in a ball and is sticky to the touch, about 7 minutes.

Place 1 cup of the dough on a clean, dry work surface. Using your hands, roll the dough across the work surface into a cylinder shape about 1 inch thick. Using a kitchen knife, cut the cylinder into 2-inch pieces. Place the dough pieces onto a parchment-lined baking sheet. Repeat with the remaining dough. Cover the baking sheet with a clean kitchen towel and set aside while you make the stew.

In a 6-quart casserole over medium heat, warm 2 tablespoons canola oil. When the oil is hot, add the onion, cabbage, and garlic and sauté until softened slightly, about 2 minutes. Add the chile paste, soy sauce, and sugar. Stir to mix, then pour in the chicken stock and kombu. Bring the broth to a simmer. Add the rice dumplings and simmer until they are heated through and the sauce has developed its flavor, 10 to 15 minutes. Quickly stir in the remaining 2 teaspoons sesame oil, the sesame seeds, and green onion. Add the mozzarella cheese.

Serve warm in wide-rimmed bowls.

OATMEAL WALNUT BREAD

We use steel-cut oats in our kitchens almost all of the time. But, the forgiving nature of this bread means that you can use any kind of leftover cooked oats here. Oats, nuts, and honey are a natural combination. The liquid content in this recipe can vary depending on the cooked oats. Adjust as necessary. We like to toast this bread and serve it topped with herbed goat cheese and fresh berries.

MAKES 2 ROUND LOAVES (BOULES)

1 cup cooked steel-cut oats

2 teaspoons active-dry yeast

2 tablespoons canola oil,
    plus more for greasing

2 cups lukewarm water

2 tablespoons honey

4 cups bread flour, plus more for dusting

2 teaspoons sea salt

½ cup toasted walnut pieces

2 tablespoons melted unsalted butter

In a large bowl, combine the cooked oats, yeast, oil, water, and 1 tablespoon of the honey and mix with a wooden spoon. In 1-cup increments, mix in the flour. Add the salt and walnuts, mixing well. Continue to mix the dough until it forms a shaggy mass. Cover the bowl with a clean kitchen towel and set aside for 15 minutes.

Turn the dough out onto a floured work surface. Knead the dough for 10 minutes. Place the dough into a greased bowl and cover with a clean kitchen towel. Let the dough rise in a warm place until it has doubled in size, about 1 hour.

Dust 2 round bread-shaping baskets lightly with flour. Punch down the dough and shape it into round balls, or boules. Place the boules into the baskets, cover with a clean kitchen towel, and let rise until doubled in size, about 40 more minutes.

Preheat the oven to 350°F. Line a large rimmed baking sheet with parchment paper.

Flip the dough onto the prepared baking sheet. Using a paring knife, score the bread across the surface with 2 angled horizontal and two angled vertical slashes.

Fill a spray bottle with water. Combine the melted butter and 1 tablespoon honey. Bake the bread until golden brown, about 45 minutes. Every 20 minutes of baking time, quickly open the oven and spray water into the bottom of the oven to create a little bit of steam. Remove the bread from the oven and brush the tops of the breads with the butter-honey mixture.

STEAMED CHOCOLATE BEET CAKES

This is a recipe we teach in our cooking school. We use Japanese butane burners to prepare it on the stove top or we cook the cakes over live fire on the beach. Cocottes are small individual-size cast-iron pots. Steaming them makes the texture of the cake spongy and light.

MAKES 6 SERVINGS

2 tablespoons unsalted butter

1 cup all-purpose flour

⅓ cup unsweetened cocoa powder

1 teaspoon baking soda

½ teaspoon sea salt

1 cup packed light brown sugar

2 large eggs

½ cup water

1 teaspoon espresso powder

½ cup sour cream

6 tablespoons unsalted butter, melted

1½ teaspoons pure vanilla bean paste
  or vanilla extract

½ cup Blueberry-Beet Jam (page 286)

Coat 6 small, individual-serving cocottes with the butter. Prepare one 6-quart casserole by placing a heatproof trivet into the bottom. Add 1½ inches of water to the pot.

Into a bowl, sift the flour, cocoa powder, and baking soda, then whisk in the salt. In a large bowl, whisk the brown sugar and eggs until slightly lightened, about 30 seconds. Whisk in the ½ cup water, espresso powder, sour cream, melted butter, and vanilla. Add the flour-cocoa mixture and gently whisk together until just combined.

Divide the batter among the buttered cocottes; it should reach about halfway up the sides. Add 1 tablespoon of the beet jam to each cocotte, dolloping it on top. Place the cocottes into the casserole, placing them onto the trivet. Place the lid onto the 6-quart casserole. It will hold four 3½-ounce coquettes, so you will need to prepare these in batches.

Bring the liquid in the casserole to a simmer. Steam the cakes over medium heat until the cakes spring back to the touch, about 13 minutes. Using kitchen towels, remove the cocottes from the casserole and keep warm. Repeat to steam the remaining cakes.

To serve, leave the cakes in the cocottes and place them onto individual serving plates. Serve warm.

SNOW-DRIED TOFU

We love the winter season, when we hang packages of tofu outside to freeze-dry. The tofu becomes airy and absorbs flavors quickly. There isn't much flavor in snow-dried tofu, so it is all about the texture and the sauces you add to the dish. We like to slice our dry tofu into 1-inch pieces and scramble them with eggs in a morning skillet, or, we tempura-fry the slices with a nutritional yeast coating. Or, we stir the tofu slices into soups for a meaty alternative.

MAKES 14 OUNCES

14 ounces pressed, medium-firm tofu   **Kitchen twine**
Cheesecloth, cut into two 12-by-6-
   inch pieces, rinsed in cold water

Cut the tofu into chunks about 4-by-2-inches each. Place each tofu chunk on a piece of damp cheesecloth and tie with twine, leaving enough twine at the end to hang it comfortably. (We leave an extra 2 feet of twine to make sure we have enough to hang the bundles from our cabin logs.)

On a cold winter day, hang the tofu outside where the birds won't get to it and it does not touch any surfaces. If you do not live in a cold climate like we do, place the cloth wrapped tofu on a plate in the freezer and turn your freezer to its coldest setting.

After 48 hours of freezing, the tofu will turn from white to a dark amber color. You can use the tofu at this point. However, we like to leave the tofu outside (or in the freezer) for 1 week to obtain the lightest texture.

After the tofu is frozen and dried to the consistency you prefer, wrap it air-tight and keep it in the freezer until you are ready to use the tofu in a dish.

SALMON SILK TOFU

This tofu dish is soft and creamy and is best served warm. Nigari flakes are a tofu coagulant made from sea water. They are available at Asian markets or online. We always use organic soy products. This recipe works best with Homemade Soymilk (page 292) or you can use store-bought soymilk by reducing it down by half to thicken. This can be served at breakfast in place of an egg custard.

MAKES 8 SERVINGS

4 cups Homemade Soymilk (page 292)

1½ teaspoons nigari flakes

1 ounce hot-smoked (kippered) salmon

Have ready eight 3-ounce (3-inch) ramekins.

Prepare one 6-quart casserole by placing a heatproof trivet into the bottom. Add 1½ inches of water to the pot. Place the casserole with the lid on the stovetop over medium heat.

Meanwhile, in a bowl, whisk together the soymilk, nigari flakes, and smoked salmon, making sure the salmon is well broken up in the soymilk mixture.

Fill the ramekins with the soymilk-salmon mixture, dividing evenly and filling each one about halfway up the sides. Remove the casserole lid, carefully transfer the ramekins to the casserole, and cover with the lid. Steam until the mixture is set, about 15 minutes. (You may need to steam the ramekins in batches.)

Carefully remove the ramekins from the casserole and set aside for 1 to 2 minutes before serving. Serve warm.

BLACK CURRANT JAM CAKE

Black currants are our jam! We have ten black currant bushes at Winterlake Lodge that keep us in this berry varietal all year long. We pick them in August and freeze them for winter use. Black currants are a favorite in both savory and sweet dishes. This cake, with an orange undertone, is a favorite to serve in the morning when it is still dark outside.

MAKES 10 TO 12 SERVINGS

Canola oil for greasing
1½ cups unsalted butter
2 cups all-purpose flour
½ cup cake flour
2 teaspoons baking powder
1¼ teaspoons sea salt
½ cup sugar
4 tablespoons honey

1 cup buttermilk
2 large eggs
½ teaspoon pure vanilla bean paste or vanilla extract
1 teaspoon finely grated orange zest
1 cup Black Currant Jam (page 286)
½ cup fresh orange juice
Plain homemade or store-bought yogurt for serving

Preheat the oven to 325°F. Grease an 8-inch round cake pan and line the pan with parchment paper.

Melt ½ cup of the butter and set aside.

In a large bowl, whisk together both flours, the baking powder, and 1 teaspoon of the salt. In a bowl, whisk together the sugar, 2 tablespoons of the honey, the buttermilk, melted butter, eggs, vanilla, and orange zest. Add the flour mixture to this buttermilk mixture, stirring just until combined.

Pour half of the batter into the prepared pan. Spoon the jam into the center of the cake, spreading it evenly, leaving at least a 1-inch border free of jam. Pour the remaining batter on top of the jam, and smooth with a spatula. Bake until the center of the cake is firm to the touch, about 1 hour. Let the cake cool completely in the pan on a wire rack. Remove the cake from the pan by inverting it onto a plate. Peel off the parchment paper.

In a small saucepan, combine the remaining 1 cup butter, remaining 2 tablespoons honey, orange juice, and remaining ¼ teaspoon salt and place over low heat until the butter is fully melted. Brush this mixture over the cake.

To serve, cut the cake into wedges, place each onto a small plate, and serve with a dollop of fresh yogurt.

VIKING BLOOD

We are proud of our Danish heritage. Perhaps that is why we can drink this hot mulled wine all winter long, wrapped up in our heavy coats and boots, out in the deep snow sitting under a million stars around the campfire.

MAKES 4 SERVINGS

2 cups water

1 cup honey

1-inch knob ginger, sliced

Two 1-inch cinnamon sticks

15 whole cloves

1 whole orange

1 whole lemon

Zest from 1 orange, removed in strips

½ cup raisins

1 cup red currants, mashed

½ cup blanched almonds, chopped

1 (750 ml) bottle dry red wine

1 cup vodka

In a large saucepan, combine the water, honey, ginger, and cinnamon sticks and place over medium-high heat. Insert the whole cloves into the whole orange and lemon and add to the pan. Add the orange strips, raisins, currants, and almonds to the saucepan. Pour in the bottle of wine. Bring the liquid to a low simmer, taking care not to boil the mixture, and simmer until aromatic, about 15 minutes.

To serve, stir in the vodka, then ladle the liquid through a small strainer into mugs and serve warm. Leave the citrus, raisins, and almonds in the remaining liquid to continue to flavor it.

CHOCOLATE SEMIFREDDO WITH BLACK CURRANT SWIRL

Semifreddo is a lovely dessert that can be made without an ice cream maker. We sometimes set the dessert in loaf pans so we can slice the individual servings. Change up the recipe with different berries, other juices, and even seaweed. We serve this at the "Ice Cream Social" party we have for the Iditarod checkers during the first night of their stay with us.

MAKES 12 SERVINGS

1 cup red currant or cranberry juice

5 ounces dark chocolate, chopped

1 tablespoon unsweetened
cocoa powder

1 cup sour cream,
at room temperature

4 large eggs, separated

½ cup sugar

1 cup heavy cream

1 teaspoon pure vanilla bean paste
or vanilla extract

½ cup chocolate chips

¼ cup Black Currant Jam (page 286)

In a small saucepan over medium heat, warm the red currant juice until simmering. In a small, heatproof bowl, combine the chocolate and cocoa powder. Pour the warm juice over the chocolate and let stand for a few minutes until melted. Stir in the sour cream and whisk until completely smooth. Transfer the mixture to a large bowl and set aside to cool slightly.

In a mixer fitted with the whisk attachment, beat the egg yolks and ¼ cup of the sugar on medium-high speed until pale in color and when you lift the whisk the batter falls slowly in a ribbon that holds its shape, about 5 minutes. Gently fold the egg yolk mixture into the cooled chocolate mixture until evenly blended.

Thoroughly wash and dry the mixer bowl and add the egg whites. Whip the whites on high speed, slowly adding the remaining ¼ cup sugar, until the whites form medium peaks, about 5 minutes. Gently fold the whipped egg whites into the chocolate mixture until evenly blended.

Wash and dry the mixer bowl and add the cream and vanilla. Whip on high speed until medium peaks form, about 5 minutes. Gently fold the whipped cream into the lightened chocolate mixture. Gently fold in the chocolate chips and red currant syrup. Divide the semifreddo into small containers that you can fit into your freezer. Cover with aluminum foil and freeze overnight or up to 6 days.

Remove the semifreddo from the freezer and let it stand at room temperature until it is slightly softened and scoopable. To serve, slice or scoop the semifreddo and serve cold.

WE LIVE ALONG A TRAIL

We are deep in winter now. The landscape and vistas in all directions at Winterlake Lodge are draped in white, with the palest of a blue hue to the snow that makes it look like some otherworldly magical painting. Winterlake is far from roads or towns, and we don't have an address other than our latitude and longitude. But, for some humans and many wild things, this place is the center of the world.

Snow dampens sound in the winter, and the quietude of the lake is sometimes the loudest thing we hear. The drama of survival outside our kitchen door plays out every day, quietly and undercover or, sometimes, in a burst of intense bravery and determination as some small, poor creature dashes into the open only to have its tiny footprints stop abruptly, surrounded by imprints of owl wings brushed in the snow. It's a wild and ancient countryside we inhabit.

Yet, there is a trail that runs right through our yard—a pronounced and packed snow road in the winter that's a small, mostly impassible overgrown swath through the woods in the summer. That's the Iditarod Trail. And there is nothing in the world quite like it.

In early winter, "trail breakers," hearty souls who volunteer with the Iditarod, come through and clear fallen branches and logs that obstruct the trail that runs for a thousand miles. The gang of men, perched on snow machines piled high with serious-looking equipment and outdoor gear, remind us of a roving band of elves or wood sprites. They drive into our yard behind the kitchen laughing, and they leave a few days later laughing. Each morning, they set out for a grueling day of work repairing the trail, each day nudging a little bit further toward McGrath and beyond. At night, the trail breakers return to the lodge and we feed them a feast at our table. We listen to their banter—tales of adventure, jokes, and laughter deep into the night as we work nearby.

One year, a trail breaker died in an avalanche between the Rohn checkpoint and Rainy Pass, to the west of us. One of our happy, laughing elves was gone, and our kitchen table fell silent. The breaker's family made tapes of his favorite music that he listened to when traveling. They had the tapes delivered to some of the checkpoints, a musical eulogy that was played in kitchens and cabins along the thousand miles of trail. It was an unusual and lovely way to remember him.

That's the Iditarod Trail. And there is nothing in the world quite like it.

Others have come here to have their ashes spread and their spirits memorialized on the trail. That's how much it means to many Alaskans, those who have traveled the thousand miles, pilots who have navigated by it, those who have merely dreamed about a life of adventure on it. One Iditarod musher's ashes are spread on our island in the middle of the lake over a patch of blueberries. A couple of years ago, a crazy gull showed up on the island, and she comes back now every summer, roosting from the top of a tall tree. A pair of loons came also to hatch their once-a-season chick just near the ash spread. It's a noisy, lively, and well-loved resting spot.

Once the trail is ready, news travels over our broad valley—and then come the buffalo hunters. We must live in one of the only places in the world where late at night, in the dead of winter, a buffalo hunter can knock on our kitchen door bearing the gift of a bloody prime piece of backstrap and slap it proudly onto our worktable. And then come the adventurers. There was a man who was walking around the world and just stopped in for a glass of water, along with

Alaska Native family on vacation visited, piled onto snow machines two people deep, including little children and a granny, as happy as if they were going to Disneyland. Two fancy Italian men in designer outfits and designer sunglasses showed up once out of nowhere, asking us if we had pasta. The Italians only had the *DeLorme Alaska Atlas and Gazetteer*, a print publication that mostly helps people navigate roadways, as a guide to get them to Nome. There was a German man in blue jeans and little gear walking to Russia. And a young couple on their honeymoon just out to see what there was to see up the trail. Another time, a couple of filmmakers stopped in on bicycles traveling over the ice to Bethel to tell the story of a gold mine being developed there. We genuinely live along a magic trail.

> It's our way of showing the human spirit can be generous and friendly and caring—and that one can be civilized even in the harshest of places.

We aren't the only ones who have lived here. Behind the lodge and down by the frog pond are a few remnants of an old cabin, now buried under snow. One summer, we found the collapsed pieces of a roofline and walls sunken into the ground, nearly impossible to see through tree roots. We dug down and found sill logs, and then we found boots and cans, a handful of bells, pots, and pans, and remnants of someone's life from long ago. We don't know who our neighbor was, but we know he decorated his cabin with a pair of moose antlers roughly wired for hanging onto his cabin wall.

We hope we feed all these visitors well that stumble upon us, way out here, where we can be an unexpected oasis of comfort against the wild. We feed them with warmth and compassion and with a kind of old-fashioned spirit that can't easily be found in non-rural places. We invite travelers into our home, and we feed them food we care about, food that is sometimes difficult for us to come by, food they might not expect. It's our way of showing the human spirit can be generous and friendly and caring—and that one can be civilized even in the harshest of places. We always have in the back of our minds that there might be adventurous travelers out on the trail, ready to find their way to our kitchen door.

So, what about our winter kitchen? It's the warmest place in the lodge and the brightest lit room for a hundred miles. The large central worktable serves as our place of business—and our place of recreation, conversations, study; our center of gravity. It's just a simple oversized table Carl built years ago, but it is just the right height, and it is plenty big enough for the kitchen team to each have our own little work areas to command. In winter, we make slow-braised dishes, lots of meaty, saucy things served with slow-risen bread. We spend free time researching far-flung food topics to explore and search through magazines for places we might like to visit. Winter is centered around root vegetables and storage goods. When we splurge and get fresh greens from Anchorage, we wrap them in blankets to get them from the runway back to the kitchen without freezing. Sometimes, at night, when we are just closing down the kitchen, we can hear wolves howling in the dark, somewhere up Wolverine Ridge. We turn off the generator and sit at the kitchen table in candlelight, listening to the soft, mournful sound of the wild.

WHITE KIMCHI SOUP

This soup warms up the coldest of winter travelers without being excessively spicy. We always have this soup on hand in the winter months. This recipe includes white cabbage kimchi, which can be purchased in many supermarkets or Asian food stores. This goes well with small bowls of white rice.

MAKES 6 SERVINGS

4 tablespoons unsalted butter

¼ pound mixed domestic mushrooms, cleaned and torn into bite-size pieces

1 tablespoon sake

Sea salt

1 green apple, peeled and cut into fine julienne

1 large yellow onion, halved and thinly sliced

1-inch knob fresh ginger, peeled and grated

1 teaspoon red pepper flakes

5 cloves garlic, thinly sliced

4 heads baby bok choy, shredded

1½ cups prepared white cabbage kimchi, thinly sliced

6 cups store-bought or homemade chicken stock

1 tablespoon honey

4 tablespoons mild miso paste

2 tablespoons liquid from kimchi

1 tablespoon soy sauce

6 ounces medium or firm tofu, cubed

Flat-leaf parsley leaves for garnish (optional)

In a 6-quart casserole over medium-high heat, melt the butter. Add the mushrooms, sake, and salt to taste. Stir in the apple, onion, ginger, and pepper flakes and simmer until the spices are aromatic and the apple and onion are tender, about 5 minutes. Add the garlic, bok choy, and kimchi and cook, stirring, until the bok choy is wilted, about 5 minutes. Add the stock and honey, reduce the heat so that the mixture just barely simmers, and cook until the flavors are fully developed, about 20 minutes.

Add the miso paste, kimchi liquid, soy sauce, and tofu. Stir gently to incorporate the ingredients.

To serve, ladle into small high-sided bowls and serve piping hot. If desired, garnish with a few parsley leaves.

FRIED SEAWEED ROLLS

In the summer, we love fresh, Vietnamese-style rolls. In the cooler weather, we enjoy these seaweed-wrapped fried snacks. Instead of the usual rice paper, we use nori for the wrapper and honestly, almost anything goes well as filling. Here, we use our Pickled Salmon Belly (page 86), but feel free to fill them as you wish. These will go fast—so make plenty. We eat these at appetizer time at the lodge or at lunch alongside other vegetable and fish dishes.

MAKES 32 APPETIZER-SIZE ROLLS

FOR THE DIPPING SAUCE

¼ cup white vinegar

½ cup soy sauce

2 teaspoons honey

2 cloves garlic, minced

2 teaspoons mild pure chile powder

1 tablespoon sesame seeds

2 green onions, thinly sliced on the bias

FOR THE ROLLS

1 cup dried cellophane noodles

½ carrot, finely julienned

8 green onions, thinly sliced on the bias

½ red onion, halved and thinly sliced

1 small bunch cilantro, roughly chopped

1 pound Pickled Salmon Belly (page 86) or cooked king salmon, flaked

1 tablespoon soy sauce

1 teaspoon sea salt

¼ teaspoon toasted sesame oil

1 teaspoon chile paste

1 teaspoon honey

8 nori seaweed sheets (7-by-8 inches)

continued on page 254

To make the dipping sauce, in a bowl whisk together the vinegar, soy sauce, honey, garlic, chile powder, sesame seeds, and green onions. Set aside.

To make the filling, bring a small saucepan of water to a boil. Add the cellophane noodles and simmer until the noodles are soft, about 7 minutes. Drain the noodles and rinse them under cold running water. Squeeze out all of the water and continue to drain. Once the noodles have most of the water squeezed out of them, place them in a bowl.

Using kitchen scissors, cut the noodles into 3-inch pieces so they are easy to eat in the seaweed roll. To the bowl with the noodles, add the carrot, green onion, red onion, and cilantro. Add the flaked salmon. Add the soy sauce, salt, sesame oil, chile paste, and honey

and toss gently with tongs until the ingredients are mixed well.

To assemble, place 1 nori sheet on a work surface with the longer side toward you. Spread some of the noodle mixture across the lower third of the nori sheet, covering the width of the sheet and leaving a 1-inch border on the upper edge of the sheet (this is similar to making sushi). Using a finger, spread water around the border of the seaweed sheet. Bringing the lower nori edge up and over the filling, tightly roll the nori around the filling into a cylinder. Repeat this step with the remaining ingredients to make 8 long rolls total. Cut each roll into 4 equal pieces to make 32 small rolls. (You can make these larger if you prefer.)

Continued on page 254

...CONTINUED
FRIED SEAWEED ROLLS

FOR THE BATTER
½ cup all-purpose flour
½ cup cornstarch
¼ teaspoon baking soda
1 teaspoon salt
1 large egg
¾ cup water

Canola oil for frying

To make the batter, in a bowl, whisk together the flour, cornstarch, baking soda, salt, egg, and water until well mixed.

Fill a 6-quart casserole with 2 quarts of oil. Place the pot over medium heat and warm the oil until it reads 350°F on a deep-frying thermometer. When the oil is hot, in batches to avoid crowding the pot, use tongs to gently place the rolls a few at a time into the batter and coat all sides. Then, gently add the battered rolls one by one to the hot oil. Fry, using metal tongs to flip them occasionally, until golden brown, 2 to 3 minutes. Remove the fried rolls with tongs and place them onto paper towels to soak off any excess oil.

Repeat to batter and fry the remaining seaweed rolls. Serve immediately with the dipping sauce.

CRANBERRY CHAMPAGNE CAKE

We save any leftover sparkling wine that has been opened to use in cooking or baking, as in this cake. This is a gorgeous, festive, wintery cake that reminds us of the tease of frozen red berries dangling down from snowy trees that we see along the trail from our lodge.

MAKES 12 TO 20 SERVINGS

FOR THE CHAMPAGNE CRANBERRIES

1½ cups superfine sugar

1 cup Champagne or sparkling wine

2 cups fresh cranberries

2 sprigs fresh rosemary

FOR THE CAKE

Canola oil for greasing

3 cups all-purpose flour

2½ teaspoons baking powder

1½ cups unsalted butter, at room temperature

2 cups granulated sugar

2 large eggs

2 tablespoons pure vanilla bean paste or vanilla extract

1 cup sour cream

½ cup buttermilk

½ cup Champagne or sparkling wine

2 cups fresh cranberries

continued on page 257

To make the Champagne cranberries, in a small saucepan, bring 1 cup of the sugar and the Champagne to a simmer over low heat. Add the cranberries and rosemary and simmer until the mixture becomes slightly syrupy, 6 to 7 minutes. Pour the mixture into a small, heatproof bowl and let cool to room temperature, about 10 minutes.

To make the cake, preheat the oven to 350°F. Line a 9-by-13-inch cake pan with parchment paper and grease well.

In a bowl, whisk together the flour and baking powder. Set aside.

In the bowl of a stand mixer fitted with the paddle attachment, combine the butter and sugar and beat on medium speed until the mixture is light and fluffy, about 2 minutes.

Scrape down the sides of the bowl with a rubber spatula. While mixing, add the eggs one at a time and mix until incorporated. Turn the mixer speed to low and add the vanilla, sour cream, buttermilk, and Champagne and mix until blended. Add the flour mixture slowly and mix until just blended. Gently fold in the cranberries. Spread the batter evenly in the prepared pan. Bake until a cake tester inserted into the center of the cake comes out clean, 35 to 40 minutes. Let the cake cool completely on a wire rack.

Continued on page 257

...CONTINUED
CRANBERRY CHAMPAGNE CAKE

FOR THE FROSTING
12 ounces (2 cups) white chocolate chips
¾ cup heavy cream
¾ cup unsalted butter, at room temperature

8 cups powdered sugar
Champagne or sparkling wine, if needed

To make the frosting, place the white chocolate chips in a heatproof bowl. In a small saucepan, warm the heavy cream over low heat until it starts to boil and then pour the cream over the white chocolate chips. Cover the bowl with a kitchen towel and let stand for 5 to 7 minutes. Uncover the bowl and whisk the chocolate-cream mixture until smooth. Set the white chocolate mixture aside until it is mostly cool, about 5 minutes. It should be thick. In a clean stand mixer bowl fitted with the whisk attachment, beat the cooled white chocolate mixture until smooth and fluffy, 2 to 3 minutes. Add the butter and beat until it is fully blended. While mixing, slowly add the powdered sugar and beat until it is light and fluffy and has the right consistency for frosting. Add a drizzle of Champagne if needed to loosen the mixture.

Remove the Champagne-cranberry mixture from the refrigerator. Remove the cranberries and rosemary from the syrup and place them onto a small cross-wire cooling rack with parchment underneath to catch any drips. Sprinkle the cranberries and rosemary with the remaining ½ cup sugar, turning them to coat all sides lightly.

Remove the cooled cake from the pan and place it on a serving platter. Spread the frosting evenly over the top and sides of the cake to coat it completely. Garnish the cake with the sugared cranberries and rosemary sprigs.

Cut the cake into squares to serve.

HOT BARLEY CEREAL

We are proud of our barley growers in Alaska. We use barley as much as we can to support our farmer friends. Plus, barley is delicious as a change from oatmeal or hot wheat cereal. Here, we add dried fruits and nuts and local syrups to make a hearty and healthful breakfast.

MAKES 4 SERVINGS

4 cups water

1 cup cream of barley cereal

½ teaspoon sea salt

1 cup toasted almonds

1 cup dried cherries

Blueberry Syrup (page 287)

Birch Butter (page 286)

1 cup whole milk, warmed

In a saucepan over medium heat, bring the water to a boil. Gradually add the barley and salt, stirring constantly. Reduce the heat to low and simmer until the cereal is the desired consistency, 1 to 3 minutes. Stir in the almonds and cherries.

Spoon the cereal into serving bowls, then drizzle with blueberry syrup and top with a pat of birch butter. Pass the milk at the table.

WINTER BISCUIT BREAKFAST SANDWICHES

These hearty breakfast biscuits made with yogurt and herbs are perfect to split, then fill with egg, cheese, and crispy breakfast bacon. When we are at the lodge in the winter, we make extras wrapped in foil and leave them near the coffee bar as grab-and-go trail snacks for the crew working outside.

MAKES 6 SANDWICHES

FOR THE BISCUITS

2 cups cake flour, plus more for dusting

1 tablespoon baking powder

1 teaspoon sea salt

1 teaspoon sugar

¼ teaspoon baking soda

6 tablespoons chilled unsalted butter, cubed

½ cup chilled buttermilk

½ cup plain yogurt

2 tablespoons fresh thyme leaves

1 large egg

1 tablespoon water

continued on page 264

Preheat the oven to 400°F. Line a baking sheet with parchment paper.

To make the biscuits, in a bowl, combine the flour, baking powder, salt, sugar, and baking soda. Using your hands, rub the butter into the flour mixture until the mixture is crumbly and the butter has been broken up into pieces about the size of peas.

In another bowl, whisk together the buttermilk, yogurt, and thyme, then add the mixture to the flour-butter mixture. Using a wooden spoon, mix the dough until it just comes together (you should be able to see chunks of butter).

Transfer the dough to a well-floured work surface. Pat or roll the dough out into a rectangle about 1 inch thick, then fold the left third of the dough over the middle third of the dough. Then, fold the right third over the center third like a letter. Repeat this process of patting or rolling out and folding the dough for a total of 3 times, adding flour as much as you need to keep dough from sticking. Finally, pat the dough into a 4-by-6-inch rectangle. Using a large kitchen knife, cut the dough into 6 square biscuits.

Continued on page 264

...CONTINUED
WINTER BISCUIT BREAKFAST SANDWICHES

TO ASSEMBLE THE SANDWICHES

2 tablespoons unsalted butter

1 clove garlic, minced

3 cups fresh baby arugula, washed

2 teaspoons apple cider vinegar

1 cup sour cream

2 tablespoons Dijon mustard

6 slices Havarti cheese

2 large red tomatoes, sliced

12 strips bacon, cooked crisp

6 eggs, fried over-medium

6 teaspoons hot pepper sauce, optional

Sea salt and freshly ground
    black pepper

Transfer the biscuits to the prepared baking sheet. In a small bowl, whisk the egg with the water to make an egg wash. Brush the egg wash on the tops of the biscuits. Bake until the biscuits are golden brown, about 15 minutes.

To assemble the sandwiches, in a small saucepan over low heat, melt the butter. Add the garlic and sauté until lightly browned, about 2 minutes. Remove from the heat.

Cut the biscuits in half crosswise. In a bowl, toss the arugula with the vinegar.

In a large sauté pan over medium heat, drizzle in the garlic butter. Add the biscuits, cut sides down, and cook until toasted, about 2 minutes. Place the biscuits toasted-side up onto a baking sheet.

In a small bowl, stir together the sour cream and the mustard. Spread a good layer of this mixture on each buttered side of the biscuits. Place a slice of Havarti cheese on 6 biscuit halves, then top each with a slice of tomato, 2 strips of bacon, ½ cup of dressed arugula, and a hot fried egg. Dot each egg with 1 teaspoon hot sauce, if desired. Top each filled biscuit with the remaining buttered biscuit halves, cut-side down. Serve right away.

SMOKED SALMON, POTATO & CARAWAY ROLLS

We like to serve these delicious rolls with a simple potato soup or a lovely salad. They can be a meal in themselves served alongside a cheese platter. Alaska farmers are famous for their potatoes and they are sold all over the world.

MAKES 16 ROLLS

2 Yukon gold potatoes, scrubbed and quartered

1 teaspoon sea salt, plus more for the cooking water

2 teaspoons honey

2½ teaspoons (1 packet) active-dry yeast

4 tablespoons unsalted butter, melted

1 clove garlic, sliced

1 cup whole milk

2 ounces hot-smoked (kippered) salmon, flaked

2 green onions, thinly sliced

4 cups all-purpose flour, plus more for dusting

1 cup light rye flour

Canola oil for greasing

1 egg white

2 tablespoons water

1 tablespoon caraway seeds

Coarse sea salt

½ cup unsalted butter

2 teaspoons granulated garlic

In a 4-quart casserole, simmer the potatoes in salted water to cover until tender, about 20 minutes. Remove 1 cup of the cooking liquid, then drain. Cool the liquid to lukewarm. Add the honey and yeast to the lukewarm liquid and set aside.

In the same casserole over low heat, melt the butter with the garlic. Add the milk, 1 teaspoon salt, and the potatoes and mash them together until smooth.

In a large bowl, combine the mashed potato mixture, smoked salmon, green onions, and foamy yeast mixture along with 1 cup of the all-purpose flour. Slowly add in the remaining 3 cups all-purpose flour and the rye flour, kneading to form a ball. Transfer the dough to a lightly floured work surface and knead until the dough is soft and pliable, about 10 minutes. Return the dough to the bowl, cover with a towel, and let it rise in a warm, draft-free place until doubled in size, about 1 hour.

Using a bench scraper, divide the dough into 16 equal portions. Roll each portion into a tight ball. Cover the balls with a towel and let them rise until doubled in size, about 30 minutes.

Preheat the oven to 375°F. Grease a baking sheet.

Move the rolls to the prepared baking sheet. Whisk together the egg white and water and brush the surface of the rolls with the mixture. Sprinkle with caraway seeds and sprinkle lightly with coarse salt. Bake the rolls until they are golden brown, about 20 minutes. Meanwhile, in a small saucepan, melt the butter and stir in the granulated garlic. Remove the rolls from the oven and brush with the melted garlic butter. Serve warm.

CAST IRON SWEET POTATO CARDAMOM BREAD

In this recipe, we use bread flour, which helps the dough to rise, and milk, which softens the dough and makes it tender. The sweet potato provides a natural sweetness, but the bread itself isn't too sweet or cloying. Sweet potatoes also last for a long time in the winter pantry. This is part of our breakfast breadbasket lineup, which we rotate through the week.

MAKES ONE 12-INCH BREAD ROUND

FOR THE DOUGH
½ cup warm milk, about 105°F
2 tablespoons active dry yeast
4 cups bread flour, plus more for dusting
¼ cup sugar
4 large eggs

2 teaspoons sea salt
¾ cup sweet potato puree
¾ cup unsalted butter,
  at room temperature
2 tablespoons finely grated orange zest

In a large bowl, mix together the milk, yeast, and ¾ cup of the bread flour. Let the mixture stand for 5 minutes.

Add the remaining flour to the bowl along with the sugar, eggs, salt, sweet potato puree, butter, and orange zest and stir until incorporated. Turn the dough out onto a well-floured work surface and knead with your hands until the dough is smooth and elastic, 4 to 5 minutes. Place the dough into a large greased bowl. Cover the bowl with a clean kitchen towel and let the dough rise in a warm, draft-free place until doubled in size, about 1 hour.

While the dough is rising, make the filling: In a small bowl, mix together the butter, brown sugar, pecans, cardamom, and cinnamon and mix well until a paste forms. Set aside.

Grease a 12-inch cast iron frying pan and set aside. Turn the dough out onto a well-floured work surface and use a rolling pin to roll it out into a 10-by-18-inch rectangle. Spread the prepared filling with a spoon evenly over the dough, leaving a 1-inch border on all sides. Roll up the dough, jellyroll fashion, starting at one long side. Turn the roll so that the seam side is down. Using a knife, cut down the center of the roll lengthwise to create 2 logs. Shape the dough in a braided fashion, crisscrossing the logs to make one big

FOR THE FILLING
¾ cup unsalted butter,
    at room temperature
1 cup firmly packed light brown sugar
1 cup chopped toasted pecans
1 teaspoon ground cardamom
1 tablespoon ground cinnamon
Canola oil for greasing

FOR THE GLAZE
1 cup powdered sugar
1 tablespoon milk
1 teaspoon lemon juice
½ teaspoon pure vanilla bean paste
    or vanilla extract

twist. Pinch the tops of the two logs together. Curl the twist into a round to fit inside the greased pan. Let the dough rise until doubled in size, about 45 minutes. (At this point, you can wrap up the pan tightly with Bee's Wrap and a clean kitchen towel and place it into the refrigerator. In the morning, remove the pan from the refrigerator, remove the wrap, and bring the dough to room temperature, about 30 minutes, before continuing.)

Preheat the oven to 350°F. While the bread is rising, make the glaze: In a small bowl, mix together the powdered sugar, milk, lemon juice, and vanilla. Set aside.

Bake the bread at 350°F for 25 minutes. Reduce the heat to 325°F and continue to bake until the bread is golden brown and firm to the touch, about 15 minutes more. If the crust is becoming too dark, cover the top of the bread with aluminum foil.

Remove the bread from the oven. Drizzle the glaze evenly over the warm bread. Let the glaze soak in a bit and then cut into sections and serve warm.

BRAISED REINDEER STEW WITH DARK BEER

This is an old-school recipe that has been in our kitchen for many years. It's warming and comforting on bitter cold winter days. Dark beer gives the stew a rich, deep flavor and color. Reindeer are also known as caribou. Substitute beef, other game, or even root vegetables for the reindeer, if you like. Serve with hearty winter bread or over wide egg noodles or roasted vegetables.

MAKES 6 SERVINGS

¼ cup canola oil

3 pounds reindeer steak, cut into 1-inch cubes

Sea salt and freshly ground black pepper

1 large slice sourdough bread, crust trimmed

2 tablespoons grainy mustard

3 tablespoons unsalted butter

1 large yellow onion, thinly sliced

2 tablespoons packed dark brown sugar

2 tablespoons red wine vinegar

2 cups dark beer

Preheat the oven to 350°F.

In a 6-quart casserole, heat the oil over medium heat. Add the reindeer meat and cook until seared on all sides, about 5 minutes per side. Transfer the seared meat to a plate and pour any excess oil from the pan. Season the meat lightly with salt and pepper. Set aside.

Spread the slice of bread with the mustard. In the same casserole, melt the butter over low heat. Add the onion and sauté until golden brown, about 5 minutes. Add the brown sugar and continue to cook until the onion is caramelized, about 7 minutes. Add the red wine vinegar and continue to sauté until the vinegar is absorbed.

Add the reindeer back to the casserole. Place the bread slice into the casserole, sticking it down into the middle of the meat. Pour in the beer. Cover the pot and put it on the center rack of the oven. Cook until aromatic and tender, about 2 hours.

Ladle into bowls and serve hot.

IT TAKES A LODGE

Neil is our expeditor and, along with Carl, does much of the construction work around the lodges. And, handles all the complicated logistics for moving freight to and from each location. He is also Mandy's husband and the love of her life. Neil can fix anything—and there is always something to fix!

Rohnen, Carly's son, is an adventurous kid, food-wise. He loves to eat smoked salmon skin, likes his meat rare, prefers his cheddar aged, and will gobble down any type of seaweed there is. His all-time favorite dish is a nice, hot bowl of noodles, which we serve him when he comes home from school ravenous.

"J" has been our winter caretaker for many years. In his off-season, he travels the world on the most outrageous and far-flung adventures you can imagine, like walking across England. It takes a certain kind of person who can be alone in an isolated and remote lodge during the winter.

Tyrone is our favorite helicopter pilot. His is also Rohnen's dad. Ty is originally from South Africa, but he has now firmly planted roots in Alaska. He is found often at Winterlake Lodge flying Robinson R-44's to our High Mountain Camp and our Glacier Camp.

Hicham is a chef who came from Morocco to live with us, changing our lives forever through his alchemy of spices and herbs, magical breads, and savory sauces and stews. He brought beautiful tagines that now fill our cooking school and remind us of him every day.

Carly, Rohnen's mom, advises us on our wellness programs, whether it is yoga on a mountaintop or meditating in the wildflower meadow. She has traveled the world in search of unique offerings to keep us centered and inspired. Carly is also a personal fitness trainer, expert fly-fisher, and massage therapist.

Carl, Kirsten's husband, has provided the inspiration for us to live the way we do. He oversees our outdoor adventures and teaches us to appreciate the natural world. Carl is the biggest cookie monster we have, and the skinniest person who cruises the kitchen for a cookie or two.

Gus is a favorite boat captain at Tutka Bay. He is always stealing the chef's kitchen bacon, so we invented a recipe for him to carry in his pocket during his long days on the water. Gus is an expert at so many things but mostly on how to be a pirate.

Tim, our R&D chef, dreams up delicious flavor combinations with both foraged and farmed edibles for both lodges. He is also an avid mountain biker and oversees our high-mountain camp at Winterlake. Tim's energy is always positive. He's an inspiration to both our culinary and adventure teams.

Taylor is the front-house manager at Winterlake Lodge. She oversees and orchestrates everything, from flower arrangements to linen counts to the lively parties in the bar every evening. Taylor embraces the natural world with the same grace and energy, and is always happy to jump into the helicopter and explore the wilds.

Wes is our guide and ops manager at Winterlake. He's a fly-fishing fanatic, a helicopter pilot, and he knows his way around the glaciers and hiking ridges of the Alaska Range better than anyone. Ask Wes to play his guitar when you are gathered around the bonfire and you'll be singing along with him all night.

Henry is Kirsten's nephew. He has been working at Tutka Bay during the summer months for several years. He has grown from a kid stumbling down the dock ramp to a vital part of our team—guiding guests, driving the boat, and basically running the whole show.

In this cookbook collection, we wanted to celebrate the people we work with and how we, as a team, navigate our lives in the wilds of Alaska. As we began to tell stories of lodge life to each other, we realized that they were often the same shared stories—a feeling of pride in our hard work, a sense of adventure, freedom living far from traditional boundaries, and a deep love and appreciation of our natural surroundings. During our collaborative process, we decided to honor a few of the people we work with by shining a spotlight on their amazing efforts. These team members rarely make an appearance in our cookbooks, but they are always supportive of our culinary projects and share our way of life.

There are so many special people in our lives, but in our family, both immediate and extended, these are the men and women who are the most important to us. We work hard side by side and they inspire us to work harder, to do what we do better. Anything is possible together.

NEIL'S BEEF STROGANOFF TOASTS

MAKES 4 SERVINGS

Neil is a picky eater by nature and some of our dishes are a little out there for him, but this is one dish we can always count on him to eat.

2 russet potatoes, scrubbed
Canola oil
Sea salt and freshly ground black pepper
½ cup plus 3 tablespoons unsalted butter
2 cloves garlic, minced
1 small sourdough baguette, halved lengthwise
1½ pounds beef tenderloin, cut into strips ½-inch thick by 2-inches long
½ pound domestic mushrooms
1 yellow onion, halved and thinly sliced
3 tablespoons all-purpose flour
3 cups store-bought or homemade beef stock
1 cup sour cream
1 small bunch fresh flat-leaf parsley, chopped
Cayenne pepper to taste

Preheat the oven to 350°F.

Using a sharp kitchen knife or mandoline, cut the potatoes into ⅛-inch thick match-sized potato sticks. Place the matchstick potatoes into cold water to rinse off some of the starch. Drain and dry well on paper towels.

In a 6-quart casserole, heat 2 quarts of canola oil until it reads 350°F on a deep-frying thermometer. In batches, drop the potatoes into the oil carefully, frying for 3 to 5 minutes until golden brown. Remove the potatoes with a mesh strainer and place them onto paper towels. Season the potatoes with salt and pepper while hot.

In a small saucepan over low heat, warm ½ cup of the butter with the garlic until melted. Scoop out some of the extra bread from the insides of the baguette to make room for the filling. Place the hollowed baguette halves onto a baking sheet. Brush the inside of the baguette halves with the garlic butter. Set aside.

Season the beef strips generously with salt and pepper. In a 6-quart casserole over medium-high heat, warm 2 tablespoons canola oil. When the oil is hot, add the beef strips, searing for 1 minute on each side. Add the mushrooms and onion and sauté until softened, about 3 minutes. Season to taste with salt and pepper. Add the remaining 3 tablespoons butter and the flour, stirring until the flour is toasted, about 1 minute. Add the beef stock and stir to mix. Bring the stock to a boil over high heat, then immediately reduce the heat until the liquid just simmers. Simmer until the sauce thickens enough to coat a spoon, about 10 minutes. Remove the pot from the heat and stir in the sour cream.

Place the baking sheet with the baguette halves in the oven and bake until golden brown, 3 to 5 minutes. Remove from the oven and place onto a serving platter.

Fill each bread half with the beef-mushroom mixture, dividing evenly. Top with the matchstick potatoes, chopped parsley, and cayenne. Cut each stuffed baguette in half crosswise. Serve hot.

ROHNEN'S UDON NOODLES

MAKES 4 TO 6 SERVINGS

Instead of the chicken stock, you can also try the Roasted Vegetable Ramen Broth (page 292) in this recipe.

FOR THE NOODLES
3 cups bread flour, plus more for dusting

⅓ cup tapioca starch

1½ teaspoons sea salt, plus salt for the cooking water

1 cup warm store-bought or homemade chicken stock

1 teaspoon toasted sesame oil, plus more
    for dressing the cooked noodles

Canola oil

FOR THE SOUP
6 cups store-bought or homemade chicken stock

1 tablespoon Thai fish sauce (nam pla)

1-inch knob fresh ginger, peeled and grated

1 clove garlic, minced

1 carrot, peeled and chopped

2 green onions, sliced

Sea salt and freshly ground black pepper

To make the noodles, in a bowl, mix together the flour, tapioca starch, and salt. Drizzle in half of the stock and mix to form a shaggy dough. Add the remaining stock and sesame oil and continue to mix until the mixture comes together in a ball. Let the dough rest in the bowl, covered with a clean kitchen towel, for 30 minutes.

Knead the rested dough by hand on a lightly oiled work surface until it is very smooth and shiny, about 10 minutes. Once the dough is smooth, form it into a tight ball and rub with a little canola oil. Place the dough ball into a clean bowl, cover with a clean kitchen towel, and let rest at room temperature for 1 to 3 hours.

Sprinkle a work surface with flour and place the dough onto it. Using a rolling pin, roll out the dough into a rectangle about ¼-inch thick. Starting from a short side, fold the dough in half and then fold in half again.

With a long, sharp knife, cut the dough crosswise into noodles about ⅛-inch wide. Separate the noodles on the work surface to prevent them from sticking together, lightly tossing them in flour if necessary.

Bring a large pot of salted water to a boil. Add the noodles and cook until they float, about 3 minutes. Remove the noodles from the water, place in a bowl, and toss with sesame oil. Cover and set aside while you make the soup.

To make the soup, in a 6-quart casserole over medium-high heat, warm the chicken stock and fish sauce. Add the ginger and garlic and bring the stock to a simmer.

Add the carrot to the stock and simmer until tender, about 5 minutes. Stir in the green onions and reserved noodles. Cook until the noodles are heated through, about 2 minutes. Season to taste with salt and pepper. Rohnen prefers mostly noodles in his bowl with very little soup broth, but the soup can be served with as much liquid as you prefer.

HICHAM'S CHAKCHOUKA SALMON BURGERS

MAKES 4 BURGERS

We left the spelling of this dish original to Hicham's notes. If you like, add some fresh arugula for crunch.

FOR THE PATTIES

1 pound boneless, skinless sockeye salmon

2 tablespoons minced fresh cilantro

2 tablespoons chopped green onion

1 clove garlic, finely minced

Juice of ½ lime

1 tablespoon soy sauce

1 teaspoon toasted sesame oil

Pinch of smoked paprika

Sea salt and freshly ground black pepper

FOR THE CHAKCHOUKA

4 tablespoons canola oil

1 yellow onion, diced

1 red bell pepper, thinly sliced

1 green bell pepper, thinly sliced

3 garlic cloves, thinly sliced

4 large tomatoes, diced

¼ cup tomato paste

2 teaspoons ground cumin

1 teaspoon paprika

1 teaspoon ground turmeric

1 teaspoon sea salt

4 large eggs

4 slices artisan bread, 1 inch thick, toasted

To make the patties, on a cutting board and using a sharp kitchen knife, mince half of the salmon as finely as you can, almost to a paste. Place the minced salmon into a bowl. Dice the other half of the salmon into medium chunks and add to the bowl. Add the cilantro, green onion, garlic, lime juice, and soy sauce and stir until mixed. Stir in the sesame oil and paprika. Season with salt and pepper to taste. Divide the mixture into 4 equal-size patties and refrigerate while you make the chakchouka.

To make the chakchouka, in a large sauté pan, warm 2 tablespoons of the oil over medium heat. When the oil is hot, add the onion, peppers, and garlic and sauté until the peppers are almost tender, about 5 minutes. Add the tomatoes, tomato paste, cumin, paprika, turmeric, and salt and simmer, uncovered, until the mixture has thickened, about 20 minutes.

Take the salmon patties out of the refrigerator and let them come to room temperature, about 15 minutes.

Using a wooden spoon, make 4 wells in the chakchouka and drop one egg into each well. Cover the pan and simmer until the eggs have set, 5 to 7 minutes.

Place a sauté pan over medium heat and add 2 tablespoons canola oil. When the oil is hot, add the salmon patties and sear until golden brown, about 2 minutes on each side.

To assemble, place one salmon patty onto each toasted bread slice. Top each patty with a scoop of the chakchouka and an egg.

HENRY'S CARDAMOM CRISP CEREAL

MAKES 6 CUPS

Henry loves cereal. He can easily eat a box of cereal a day. This is a recipe Mandy developed especially for him.

¼ cup granulated sugar

2 teaspoons ground cinnamon

¼ teaspoon plus ⅛ teaspoon ground cardamom

1 teaspoon pure vanilla bean paste or vanilla extract

½ cup water

½ cup canola oil

2 tablespoons honey

1½ cups all-purpose flour

½ cup whole-wheat flour

1½ teaspoons baking soda

¼ teaspoon sea salt

¼ cup unsalted butter

½ cup superfine sugar for finishing

Cold milk or yogurt for serving

Preheat the oven to 375°F.

In a bowl, whisk together the granulated sugar, 1 teaspoon of the cinnamon, ¼ teaspoon of the

cardamom, the vanilla, water, canola oil, and honey. Set aside.

In the bowl of a stand mixer fitted with the paddle attachment, combine the flours, baking soda, and salt. Turn the mixer on low speed, then slowly add the sugar-spice-oil mixture and mix until incorporated. The dough should be the consistency of cookie dough.

Divide the dough into half and place each half on a piece of parchment paper. Place another piece of parchment paper on top and use a rolling pin to roll out each dough half to a rectangle about ⅛-inch thick. Peel off the top sheet of parchment.

Melt the butter and brush it over the dough. Using a paring knife, score the dough halfway through its thickness into 1-inch squares. Carefully transfer each section of scored dough, still on the bottom piece of parchment, to a baking sheet. Place the sheets in the oven and bake until the squares are golden brown, 10 to 15 minutes.

While the cereal squares are baking, in a small bowl, combine the superfine sugar, remaining 1 teaspoon cinnamon, and the remaining ⅛ teaspoon cardamom.

Remove the squares from the oven. While still hot, sprinkle the sugar-spice mixture over the top. Let the squares cool completely, then break up the squares at the score marks and store in an airtight container until ready to serve. Serve with cold milk or yogurt.

CARL'S VITAMIN C'S

MAKES 24 COOKIES

These are "Vitamin Carl" cookies. This cookie combines two of Carl's favorite snacks: chocolate and pretzels. If he had his way, all cookies would be made with dark chocolate, but we're putting semisweet in this recipe because that is how we prefer them—sorry, Carl.

2 cups all-purpose flour
1½ cup rolled oats
¼ cup cake flour

¼ cup unsweetened cocoa powder, sifted
¾ teaspoon baking soda
½ teaspoon sea salt, plus more for sprinkling
1 cup chilled unsalted butter, cut into cubes
1 cup packed light brown sugar
½ cup granulated sugar
2 large eggs
1 teaspoon pure vanilla bean paste or vanilla extract
2 cups semisweet chocolate chips
1 cup dried cherries
1 cup chopped walnuts
½ cup coarsely crushed pretzels

In a bowl, combine the all-purpose flour, oats, cake flour, cocoa powder, baking soda, and salt. Stir until combined. Set aside.

In the bowl of a stand mixer fitted with the paddle attachment, cream together the butter and both sugars on medium speed until light and fluffy, about 2 minutes. On low speed, add the eggs one at a time, mixing well after each addition. Mix in the vanilla.

Still mixing on low speed, slowly add the flour mixture and mix just until combined. Add the chocolate chips, cherries, walnuts, and pretzel bits and mix until combined. Cover the dough with a Bee's Wrap or a kitchen towel and refrigerate for at least 20 minutes or up to overnight.

Preheat the oven to 325°F. Line 2 baking sheets with parchment paper.

Using a small cookie scoop, scoop out cookie dough balls onto the prepared baking sheets, leaving 2 inches between each cookie. Using your fingers, lightly press each cookie dough to flatten it. Bake until the cookies are firm and cooked through, 10 to 12 minutes.

Remove the cookies from the oven, sprinkle lightly with sea salt, and let cool completely on a wire rack before serving.

J'S CARETAKER GRANOLA

MAKES 5 CUPS

Mandy makes a big batch of this granola for J to enjoy as he revels in the quiet and private world of being alone at the lodge.

2 cups quick-cooking oats
2 cups rolled oats
1 cup walnuts, broken into small pieces
1 teaspoon ground cinnamon
½ teaspoon sea salt
1 cup unsalted butter
½ cup packed light brown sugar
¼ cup honey
Canola oil
1 cup dried cherries

Preheat the oven at 350°F.

In a large bowl, combine both types of oats, walnuts, cinnamon, and salt and mix well. In a small saucepan over medium heat, melt the butter, brown sugar, and honey together, stirring until smooth. Pour the mixture over the oat mixture and mix with a wooden spoon until all of the oats are well coated.

Line a large rimmed baking sheet with parchment paper. Grease the sheet well. Spread the oat mixture in an even layer over the baking sheet with a wooden spoon. Put the baking sheet in the oven and bake until toasted and golden brown, about 35 minutes, stirring once halfway through baking time.

Remove the granola from the oven and stir in the dried cherries. Let cool completely before serving.

Store the granola in an airtight container for up to 30 days.

TIM'S KOJI MARINATED MUSHROOMS

Tim made these mushrooms for us during our James Beard dinner in New York and they were delicious. Admittedly, this is a chef recipe, but it's a fun and delicious one to try in your home kitchen.

Koji is used to make miso, sake, and other Japanese condiments and drinks. Koji and shio koji have a sweet, mellow taste. You can find these ingredients from online sources or in Asian markets.

MAKES 4 APPETIZER SERVINGS

1 cup shio koji
⅓ cup koji powder
¼ cup extra-virgin olive oil
1 cup mixed wild mushrooms, cleaned and halved lengthwise
⅓ cup demiglace
2 tablespoons orange marmalade
2 tablespoons Chinese black vinegar
Canola oil
3 tablespoons unsalted butter
4 tablespoons salmon roe
Pinch of dried enoki mushrooms

In a bowl, whisk together the shio koji, koji powder, and olive oil. Put the mushrooms in a reusable zippered plastic bag and pour over the koji mixture. Seal the bag and let the mixture stand at room temperature for about 12 hours.

Remove the mushroom mixture from the bag and pat the mushrooms dry with paper towels. Place a rack into a rimmed baking sheet and place the mushrooms on the rack so that they're not touching. Set the mushrooms aside to air-dry for about 4 hours.

In a small saucepan, combine the demiglace, marmalade, and Chinese vinegar. Place over low heat to warm through.

Place a cast iron pan over medium-high with a little oil to coat the bottom. Once warm, add the butter and put the mushrooms into the pan. Reduce the heat to medium-low and cook the mushrooms, basting them with the melted butter from the pan, until they start to caramelize, about 5 minutes. Turn over the mushrooms, turn off the heat, and continue to baste the mushrooms until they are heated through, about 3 minutes. Remove the mushrooms from the pan and drain on paper towels.

To serve, spoon about 2 tablespoons of the demiglace mixture into the center of each of 4 small plates. Add ½ tablespoon each of the salmon roe to the plates.

Divide the sliced fermented mushrooms among the plates, placing them around the sauce. Garnish with the dried enoki mushrooms.

TY'S
MILK & HONEY TART

MAKES 8 TO 10 SERVINGS

This is Ty's recipe, which, among many, he has passed along from his homeland. Ty sprinkles his tarts with cinnamon, but we like to add available fruits on top.

2¼ cups whole milk
2 tablespoons unsalted butter
½ teaspoon freshly grated nutmeg
2 tablespoons all-purpose flour
2 tablespoons cornstarch
¼ cup sugar
½ tablespoon pure vanilla bean paste or vanilla extract
½ tablespoon almond extract
2 large eggs
¼ cup honey
1 baked Tart Shell (page 294)

Place a saucepan over medium heat. Add the milk, butter, and nutmeg. Bring the mixture just to a boil and then remove from the heat.

In a heatproof bowl, mix together the flour, cornstarch, sugar, vanilla, and almond extract. Whisk in the eggs and honey until smooth. While whisking, pour the hot milk mixture into the flour and egg mixture, mixing well. Pour the mixture back into the saucepan over low heat. Cook the mixture, stirring constantly with a whisk, until the milk mixture is thickened, about 10 minutes. Remove the pan from the heat. Pour the mixture into the baked tart shell. Let cool for about 10 minutes.

Put the tart into the refrigerator, uncovered, and chill until ready to serve.

Cut the tart into wedges to serve.

GUS'S
POCKET BACON

MAKES 24 PIECES

Mandy made this expanded version of a piece of bacon for Gus. Mandy's instructions for this recipe are, "Have available for Gus to swoosh by the kitchen and grab one on his way out to an adventure."

2 cups raw cashews
12 strips thick-cut smoked bacon, cooked until crisp
1 cup pitted dates
1 cup dried cranberries or red currants
¼ cup unsweetened cocoa powder
2 teaspoons sea salt

Put the cashews in a food processor and process until they form a rough paste. Add the bacon and pulse to break it up into small chunks; take care that you don't puree it too much.

Remove the cashew-bacon mixture from the processor and set the mixture aside in a bowl. Add the dates and cranberries to the processor and blend them into a paste, working in batches if necessary.

Add the date-cranberry mixture to the bowl with the cashew-bacon mixture and stir together until mixed. Add the cocoa powder and salt and stir until mixed.

Pour the dough out onto a sheet of parchment paper and place another sheet of parchment on top. Using a rolling pin, roll out the dough into a rectangle ½-inch thick and refrigerate until firm, about 2 hours.

Cut the mixture into 2- by 1-inch pieces. Wrap the pieces in foil or enclose in parchment snack bags. The pocket bacon will keep for up to 7 days in the refrigerator.

TAYLOR'S MISO-MARINATED FRIED CHICKEN

MAKES 6 SERVINGS

Taylor is a people person and a collaborator. She loves game nights with the staff. This chicken recipe is an interesting choice for a late-night gathering.

2 pounds boneless, skin-on chicken thighs
½ cup light miso
1 tablespoon grated fresh ginger
1 tablespoon minced garlic
½ teaspoon paprika
2 teaspoons soy sauce
2 green onions, thinly sliced
Canola oil for deep frying
¼ cup all-purpose flour
¼ cup cornstarch
4 tablespoons honey
Sea salt and freshly ground black pepper

In a bowl, combine the chicken, miso, ginger, garlic, ¼ teaspoon of the paprika, soy sauce, and green onions. Massage the chicken in the marinade for 20 seconds. Cover the bowl and refrigerate for 8 to 12 hours.

Pull the chicken out of the refrigerator and let come to room temperature before frying, about 10 minutes.

Pour 2 inches of canola oil into a 6-quart casserole. Warm the oil over medium heat until it reads 325°F on a deep-frying thermometer.

Combine the flour, cornstarch, remaining ¼ teaspoon paprika, and salt and pepper to taste. When the oil is almost ready, pour the flour-cornstarch mixture into the bowl with the chicken. Mix to coat the chicken well.

Gently drop the coated chicken pieces into the hot oil and fry until golden brown, about 11 minutes, making sure the chicken is cooked on all sides. Using tongs, transfer the chicken to a wire rack set over a baking sheet to drain.

Drizzle the fried chicken with honey and season with salt and pepper to taste. Serve hot.

WES'S FERMENTED CARROT HOT SAUCE

MAKES ABOUT 2 CUPS

Wes practically drinks the peri-peri hot sauce we always have in the kitchen. This is our own version. Use this sauce on everything from fish to vegetables to rice. It goes well as a secret ingredient splash into soups and sauces.

6 cups warm filtered water
2 tablespoons fine sea salt
¼ pound habanero chiles
4 bird's eye chiles
4 large carrots, thinly sliced
6 black garlic cloves
2 shallots, sliced
One 5-by-12-inch sheet nori seaweed
½ green apple, sliced
¼ cup apple cider vinegar
Honey to taste (optional)

In a bowl, combine the warm water and salt, stirring to dissolve the salt.

Wearing gloves, cut the habanero and bird's-eye chiles in half and remove the seeds (for less heat) or leave some or all of the seeds for extra-hot sauce. There's no need to remove the stems.

Layer both chiles, the carrots, black garlic, shallots, and seaweed into a glass pitcher or large glass jar. Pour the saltwater into the pitcher or jar, pressing the vegetables down under the liquid. (If you need to add more saltwater, remember to use the ratio of 1 teaspoon salt per 1 cup of water.)

Put the sliced apple on top of the vegetables, which will weigh them down even more—it's important that the vegetables are completely submerged under the brine. Place the pitcher or jar on a baking sheet to collect any liquid that may spill from expansion. Cover the pitcher with a kitchen towel and leave on the kitchen counter until the brine appears slightly cloudy, about 6 days.

Strain the brine from the solids, reserving the brine. Transfer all of the solids to a blender. Add 1 cup of the brine and blend until completely smooth. Add the vinegar and the optional honey, if you prefer a sweeter hot sauce, and blend to mix, adding more brine if desired to adjust the thickness.

Transfer the sauce to small glass jars, leaving room for some expansion, cover lightly, and refrigerate until ready to use. The flavors will continue to develop and get more complex over time. The sauce will keep for up to 3 months in the refrigerator.

CARLY'S WILD VIOLET JELLY

MAKES 4 HALF-PINT JARS

Carly loves to gather wildflowers for the kitchen. This is a lovely scarlet jelly that is one of our treasures of early springtime. Use any edible garden flowers with this process as long as they are chemical-free. Some online sources sell edible flowers.

3 cups organic violet petals
4 cups boiling water
½ cup fresh lemon juice
3 cups sugar
6 tablespoons liquid pectin

Place the violet petals in a heatproof bowl. Pour the boiling water over the petals. Let the flowers steep, covered with a kitchen towel, until aromatic and the water is lightly colored, about 1 hour.

Strain the liquid from the steeped flowers into a bowl. Add the lemon juice.

Transfer the violet liquid mixture to a saucepan and add the sugar. Bring the liquid to a boil over high heat. Add the pectin and continue to boil for 1 minute. Skim any foam that forms on the top of the mixture.

Carefully pour the hot liquid into sterilized canning jars. Seal the jars according to the canning jar manufacturer's instructions. Refrigerate opened jars of the jelly and use within 1 month.

THE PANTRY

sn't "pantry" a lovely word? We have always enjoyed having an intriguing and creative pantry wherever we happen to be. We even taught a class once at the University of Alaska, Anchorage on how to assemble an interesting and active home pantry space. We rotate foods twice a year so things don't get too cluttered or dusty, and we keep a tape label maker at hand to identify jars of this and that. We reach constantly for the spices, dried herbs, sauces, and bits of wonder that make our food look and taste beautiful. A well-thought out pantry can be your best kept kitchen secret.

BIRCH BUTTER

MAKES 2 CUPS

Birch syrup has a particular flavor. Its strong taste goes a long way, but we find this butter enhances many of our dishes, from vegetables to fish to desserts to breakfast dishes.

1 cup unsalted butter, at room temperature
½ cup packed light brown sugar
½ cup birch syrup
½ teaspoon sea salt

In the bowl of a stand mixer fitted with the paddle attachment, combine the butter, brown sugar, syrup, and salt. Mix on low speed until well blended. Transfer the butter to a sheet of waxed paper, using a rubber spatula to get it all out of the bowl. Roll the butter into a log and wrap securely. Keep the butter in the refrigerator for up to 5 days.

BLACK CURRANT JAM

MAKES FIVE 8-OUNCE JARS

Here's another pantry staple we hope to never be without. We use it as a delicious spread on morning sourdough toast. We also fill cakes with this, and we sometimes drop it into cookie and brownie batter.

6 cups fresh black currants
3 cups sugar
1 cup apple cider
Juice of 1 lemon

Clean the currants and remove any bits of stem or leaf. Thoroughly rinse the currants through a colander and drain well.

In a large saucepan, combine the currants, sugar, cider, and lemon juice. Crush the currants with the back of a spoon. Bring the mixture to a hard boil over high heat, then reduce the heat so that the mixture is at a low simmer. Cook until the jam is just beginning to gel, the currant skins are soft, and the mixture has thickened. The timing can vary depending on the fruit, from 30 minutes up to a couple of hours.

To test if the jam is thick enough, put a tablespoon of the hot jam onto a chilled plate. Put the plate in the freezer until the jam is room temperature. Run your finger through the middle of the mixture. The two sides should combine together again immediately.

Skim off any foam from the top of the jam with a large spoon. Transfer the hot jam mixture to clean 8-ounce canning jars and store in the refrigerator up to 1 week. Alternately, you can sterilize the jam using the water bath method according to the canning jar manufacturer's instructions.

BLUEBERRY-BEET JAM

MAKES 2 CUPS

Beets grow well in Alaska and we love them for savory and sweet applications, such as slathered onto breakfast breads, used in baked goods, made into ice creams, used for curing salmon, and more. We even use beet juice sometimes to color liquids to be more scarlet.

2½ cups beet juice
1¼ cups blueberries
1 tablespoon honey
1½ tablespoons chia seeds
6 tablespoons liquid pectin

In a nonmetallic (cast enamel or ceramic) saucepan, combine the beet juice, blueberries, honey, and chia seeds. Turn the heat to medium and cook until the mixture is reduced by half and the liquid coats the back of a spoon, about 5 minutes.

Whisk in the pectin, bring the mixture to a boil, and cook for 1 minute. Remove the mixture from the heat and let cool to room temperature. Transfer the jam to a clean glass canning jar with a lid. Refrigerate for up to 1 week.

BLUEBERRY CURD

MAKES 1½ CUPS

1 cup freshly pressed blueberry juice

Finely grated zest of 1 lemon

1 large egg

2 large egg yolks

¼ cup sugar

4 tablespoons unsalted butter, cubed, at room temperature

1 teaspoon pure vanilla bean paste or vanilla extract

Pinch of sea salt

In a small saucepan over medium-high heat, bring the berry juice to a simmer. Cook until the juice has reduced to about ¾ cup, about 5 minutes. Remove from the heat, stir in the lemon zest, and let cool to room temperature.

In a bowl, whisk together the egg, egg yolks, and sugar. While whisking constantly, add the cooled juice mixture into the egg mixture in a steady stream until well incorporated.

Fit a fine-mesh strainer over a bowl and set aside. Pour the egg-juice mixture back into the small saucepan. Place over medium heat and cook, stirring slowly, until the mixture has thickened to a pudding-like consistency, about 8 minutes.

Pour the mixture through the strainer into the bowl to strain out the zest and any bits of cooked egg. Stir the butter, vanilla, and salt into the strained mixture and mix until the butter is completely melted and the curd is smooth. Let the curd cool completely, then store in the refrigerator until ready to use, up to 1 week.

BLUEBERRY SYRUP

MAKES 4 CUPS

This syrup is always in our pantry. Always. And, if it isn't, Kirsten isn't happy. If you don't live in a place that has local blueberries, buy organic frozen ones from the market and make this anyway. Use it for salad dressing, on pancakes, brushed on salmon (or other) bacon, in cakes, in muffins, and even in happy hour cocktails.

5 cups blueberries

4 cups water

1 cup granulated sugar

1 cup packed light brown sugar

1 cup fresh orange juice

2 tablespoons honey

1 tablespoon cornstarch

Juice of 1 lemon

In a saucepan over low heat, combine the blueberries with 1 cup of the water. Crush the berries with a whisk and bring the mixture to a simmer. Simmer the berries until they are broken down and soft, about 10 minutes. Strain the berries through a fine-mesh strainer into a small bowl, pressing to remove all of the juice from the berries. Discard the solids.

In a clean saucepan over medium heat, combine the sugars, orange juice, honey, and the remaining 3 cups water and bring to a boil, stirring to dissolve the sugar. Reduce the heat so that the mixture just simmers and continue to cook until the volume has reduced slightly, about 20 minutes.

Place the cornstarch into a bowl. Add the blueberry juice and lemon juice and whisk until there are no clumps. While whisking, slowly pour the blueberry mixture into the orange juice-honey mixture and simmer until well mixed, about 1 minute. Let the syrup cool and store in sealed canning jars for up to 6 months.

HOMEMADE BUTTERMILK

MAKES 1 CUP

We always include buttermilk in our must-have lodge pantry lists to use in baking and breads. But, if we don't have fresh buttermilk on hand, we use this quick method.

1 tablespoon lemon juice
1 cup heavy cream

In a jar, combine the lemon juice and cream. Cover tightly and let stand at room temperature for about 15 minutes. Refrigerate until needed. The buttermilk will keep for up to 1 week.

SMOKED, SALTED CARAMEL SAUCE

MAKES ABOUT 2 CUPS

2 cups sugar
¼ cup unsalted butter, at room temperature, cut into pieces
1 cup heavy cream
1 tablespoon smoked sea salt, plus more for sprinkling
1 teaspoon pure vanilla bean paste or vanilla extract

Heat the sugar in a heavy-bottomed saucepan over medium heat until the sugar is golden amber in color and completely melted, about 5 minutes. If you wish to use a candy thermometer, sugar caramelizes at 350°F, but we usually just watch for the golden color. Whisk in the butter. Off the heat, carefully whisk in the cream (it may splatter), the salt, and vanilla extract. Remove the saucepan from the heat to cool the mixture for a few minutes. You can pour the cooled caramel sauce into a glass jar for storage and cover the jar with a lid. The sauce will last for up to 2 weeks in the refrigerator. Reheat gently before using.

CASHEW SAUCE

MAKES 2 CUPS

Use this versatile, creamy mixture as a dipping sauce or thin it out with a little bit of rice wine vinegar as a dressing. Sweet soy sauce is worth having in the pantry to drizzle onto hot rice, add to sweet or savory sauces, or brush onto salmon. Add more or use less water to reach your desired consistency.

1 cup cashew butter
½ cup rice vinegar
¼ cup yuzu juice
¼ cup sweet soy sauce
¼ cup water
1 tablespoon minced garlic
1-inch knob fresh ginger, peeled and minced
½ tablespoon chile paste

In a bowl, combine the cashew butter, vinegar, yuzu, sweet soy, water, garlic, ginger, and chile paste. Use a whisk or immersion blender to blend until all is well incorporated. Store the sauce in a glass canning jar, covered, in the refrigerator for up to 3 days.

CINNAMON WHIPPED CREAM

MAKES ABOUT 2 CUPS

1 cup heavy cream
½ teaspoon pure vanilla bean paste or vanilla extract
½ cup powdered sugar
¼ teaspoon ground cinnamon

In the bowl of a stand mixer fitted with the whisk attachment, whip the cream and vanilla until it starts to thicken, about 2 minutes. While mixing, slowly add the powdered sugar and the cinnamon. Whip until light and fluffy, another 1 minute.

DUCK CONFIT

MAKES 4 LEGS

This is a regular pantry item in all of our kitchens. We like to shred the confit and add it to almost everything, but particularly winter bean dishes.

4 skin-on, bone-in duck legs
4 tablespoons sea salt
1 teaspoon whole juniper berries, toasted and crushed
6 cups duck fat
4 sprigs fresh thyme
2 bay leaves

6 cloves garlic
1 shallot, sliced

Rinse the duck legs under cold water and dry completely. Place the duck legs in a bowl. Rub the salt and the crushed juniper on all sides of the duck. Place a piece of Bee's Wrap directly on top of the duck legs, then place another mixing bowl on top to weigh the legs down. Refrigerate the duck legs for 2 days to season them well.

Remove the duck legs from the refrigerator and rinse off all of the salt and spice. Pat dry. Preheat the oven to 200°F.

In a large, 6-quart casserole over medium heat, melt the duck fat. Add the duck legs, thyme sprigs, bay leaves, garlic, and shallot and place in the oven. Roast until the duck legs are tender and fall off the bone, about 3 hours.

With a fish spatula, remove the duck legs and set aside. Strain the duck fat through a fine-mesh strainer. Lay the duck legs in a shallow, non-metallic dish and pour the fat over the top until it covers the legs. Cover and refrigerate for up to 1 month.

DUMPLING WRAPPERS

MAKES ABOUT 25

Use these for Chinese-flavored dumplings or branch out to other flavor palettes. Peanut butter and jelly dumplings? Maybe not, but how about wild berry and ricotta cheese? Or, dumplings filled with roasted winter squash and Duck Confit (page 288)?

⅔ cup water
2 cups all-purpose flour, plus extra for dusting
1 teaspoon sea salt
Canola oil for kneading
Cornstarch for dusting

In a small saucepan, bring the water to a boil. In a heatproof bowl, stir together the flour and salt. Pour the boiling water into the flour mixture all at once and stir into a rough ball.

Once cooled slightly, knead the dough on a lightly oiled work surface until it is smooth and elastic, 6 to 8 minutes. Return the dough to a lightly oiled bowl, cover the bowl with a clean kitchen towel, and set aside for about 30 minutes.

Cut the dough in half with a kitchen knife and form each half into a ball. Using your hands, roll each dough ball back and forth across the oiled work surface to make a rope about 18 inches long. Transfer the ropes to a work surface that's well-dusted with flour and use a knife to cut each rope into ¾-inch lengths. Roll each dough length into a ball, then flatten out the ball with the palm of your hand into a disk.

Using a small rolling pin, roll each disk into a round about 3 inches in diameter. Cover the prepared wrappers with Bee's Wrap or a dry clean towel while making additional skins. Dust each wrapper with a light coating of cornstarch to prevent sticking together and wrap tightly to use in the future. The dumpling wrappers can be refrigerated for up to 1 week or frozen for up to 3 months.

ESPRESSO WHIPPED CREAM

MAKES ABOUT 2 CUPS

This take on whipped cream can be an interesting addition to a dessert plate. At the lodge, we serve it in a small bowl (kept on ice) by the coffee station where we have hot chocolate ready to go on winter days.

1 cup chilled heavy cream
¼ cup packed light brown sugar
1 teaspoon pure vanilla bean paste or vanilla extract
1 teaspoon instant espresso powder
¼ teaspoon sea salt

In the bowl of a stand mixer fitted with the whisk attachment, whip the heavy cream on medium speed until it starts to thicken, about 2 minutes. Add the brown sugar, vanilla, and espresso powder. Continue to whip until medium peaks form, about 5 minutes. Cover and refrigerate until ready to use.

FERMENTED HONEY

MAKES 2 CUPS

This is a condiment that you will come to love. We put it in everything! The sweet with the acid makes a complementary flavor combination. Honey lasts forever, so don't be worried about having too much around.

1½ cups honey
½ cup water
1 tablespoon lemon juice

In a clean canning jar, combine the honey, water, and lemon juice. Stir until just combined. Seal the jar loosely and let the honey ferment for 2 to 7 days in a warm place before using. Tighten the jar lid and store the honey on a pantry shelf. The fermented honey will keep for up to 6 months.

GRANULATED GARLIC

MAKES ABOUT 1 CUP

Our dear farmer friend Lori grows lots of garlic. We take her lovely Alaska-grown garlic and preserve it through dehydration. Granulated garlic is handy in some recipes where we need the flavor to mix easily. Three average-sized garlic heads should make about 1 cup granulated garlic, but it varies depending on the size of the cloves.

3 heads garlic, cloves separated and peeled

Preheat the oven to 200°F. Line a baking sheet with parchment paper.

Cut the garlic into thin slivers as close to the same thickness as possible. While working, spread the garlic slivers onto the lined baking sheet in a single layer. Place the baking sheet onto the center rack of the oven and bake until very dry. The drying process can take as little as 1 hour and as long as overnight, depending on the age and moisture content of the garlic. (Alternatively, follow the manufacturers' instructions to use a food dehydrator.)

When the garlic is dried, pulse it in a food processor until the garlic is in small, coarse grains.

Store the granulated garlic in a clean and dry airtight glass jar with a tight-fitting lid. The garlic will keep for up to 6 months.

KELP PICKLES

MAKES 2 CUPS

We like the idea that bull kelp has been used by Alaskans for hundreds of years. Of course, our pickles are an update, but nonetheless, we feel a connection with the past and with the ocean when we add these to the table. Look for bull kelp along the shoreline after a big winter storm—or, perhaps find it online. If you can't find bull kelp, use a favorite vegetable.

One 12-inch strip bull kelp
4 cups water
2 cups apple cider vinegar
1 cup sugar
2 cloves garlic
1 teaspoon whole cloves
2 teaspoons fennel seeds
1 teaspoon mustard seeds
1 teaspoon black peppercorns
½ teaspoon turmeric
½ teaspoon red pepper flakes
1-inch knob fresh ginger, peeled and sliced
1 small red onion, halved and thinly sliced
1 teaspoon coarse sea salt

Put the kelp in a large bowl of cold water and clean it to remove any shell fragments. Using a vegetable peeler, peel the rough outer skin from each section. Then, cut each section into ¼-inch rings. Rinse the rings in cold water, changing the water several times, to mellow the ocean water flavor.

In a 4-quart casserole, combine the water, vinegar, sugar, garlic, cloves, fennel seeds, mustard seeds, peppercorns, turmeric, red pepper flakes, ginger, red onion, and salt. Bring the mixture just to a boil over high heat, then reduce the heat so that the liquid just simmers. Add the kelp rings. Simmer for about 5 minutes. The kelp won't change in texture, but the color may brighten slightly. You can strain the liquid or use it unstrained.

Transfer the kelp rings and cooking liquid to clean canning jars. Sterilize in a water bath method according to canning jar manufacturer or keep in the refrigerator, covered but unsealed. Let the pickles stand for at least 1 week before using. The pickles will keep for up to 2 months unsealed, and 6 months canned.

POTATO TART SHELL

MAKES ONE 10-INCH TART SHELL

2 cups all-purpose flour, plus extra for dusting
½ cup cold butter, cut into cubes
1 red potato, scrubbed and shredded
1 large egg yolk
3 tablespoons ice water

Place the flour and butter into a food processor and pulse until the mixture forms pea-size pieces. In a small bowl, stir together the shredded potato, egg yolk, and ice water. Add this mixture to the food processor and pulse until the mixture just comes together. Form into a disk, wrap in Bee's Wrap, and chill for 15 minutes.

Place the dough on a lightly floured work surface. Using a rolling pin, roll the chilled dough to a round ¼-inch thick. Carefully transfer the dough to a greased 10-inch fluted tart pan with a removable bottom and gently press the dough into the sides. Trim the edges and freeze the trim for future use. Refrigerate the dough for 15 minutes.

Preheat the oven to 350°F.

Remove the tart pan from the refrigerator and cover the dough with parchment paper. Add dried beans (or other pie weights) on top of the paper and press the paper and weights into the dough edges. Bake for 20 minutes, then carefully lift out the beans and paper. Return the tart shell to the oven and bake until light brown and dry to the touch, about 10 more minutes. Remove from the oven and let cool completely on a wire rack.

HOMEMADE PUFF PASTRY

MAKES 1 POUND PASTRY

Puff pastry is easy to make and has the fresh taste of butter, so why buy store-bought that is often made with oil and has a weird oily mouth-feel? We use this recipe for our Salmon Hand Pies (see page 84).

4 cups bread flour, plus more for dusting
2 teaspoons sea salt
2 cups cold unsalted butter, cut into ½-inch cubes
½ cup cold water, plus more if needed

In large bowl, sift together the flour and salt. Add in the cold butter, rubbing the flour and butter together between your fingers until it is in pea-sized pieces. Make a well in the center of flour mixture. Pour in the cold water and mix with your hands until you have a firm, rough dough, adding additional water if needed. Cover and refrigerate the dough for about 20 minutes.

Turn out the dough onto a lightly floured work surface and knead gently. Using a rolling pin, roll out the dough into a 12-by-18-inch rectangle. Fold the left third of the dough over the second third, then fold the right third over like you are folding a letter. Turn the dough 90 degrees on the work surface. Again, roll the dough into 12-by-18-inch rectangle. Fold the dough into thirds like a letter one more time. Divide the dough in half and wrap in a clean, dry kitchen towel. Refrigerate for at least 20 minutes before using. Or, wrap the dough tightly in Bee's Wrap and freeze until ready to use, up to 3 months.

RHUBARB CHUTNEY

MAKES ABOUT 2 QUARTS

Trust us: Just make this. After you try it, you'll always want to have this in your pantry. We put rhubarb chutney on our cheese board every evening at appetizer hour. We serve it almost always with our salmon and halibut burgers, and even put it on the to-go turkey sandwiches at the café.

2 pounds red rhubarb, cut into
** ½-inch pieces (about 6 cups)**

2 cups dark red cherries, pitted and quartered

1 large red onion, diced

1½ cups dried blueberries

2 cloves garlic, minced

1 knob fresh ginger, peeled and minced

1 teaspoon red pepper flakes

2 cups packed light brown sugar

1 cup cherry juice

2 cups apple cider vinegar

¼ cup honey

In a large saucepan, combine the rhubarb, cherries, onion, dried blueberries, garlic, ginger, pepper flakes, brown sugar, and cherry juice. Bring the mixture to a boil over medium-high heat, then reduce the heat to medium-low and simmer for 30 minutes. Add the vinegar and honey. Continue to simmer until the mixture is thickened, about 30 more minutes.

Cool the chutney and store in 2 clean glass quart-size canning jars and store in the refrigerator, covered, for up to 1 month. Or, sterilize with the water bath method according to jar manufacturer's recommendations. Canned chutney will last for 6 months.

ROASTED VEGETABLE RAMEN BROTH

MAKES ABOUT 6 CUPS

We enjoy vegetable ramen and make this broth when we want something without the pork that is typical of ramen broths. It's lovely to use for other dishes besides ramen as well, such as the broth for Rohnen's Udon Noodles (see page 275).

2 small eggplants, quartered lengthwise

3 yellow onions, unpeeled and quartered

2 carrots, peeled and cut into 1-inch dice

¼ head green cabbage

6 cloves garlic, smashed

2-inch knob fresh ginger, cut into ¼-inch slices

Canola oil

2 tablespoons Fermented Honey (page 290)

Stems from 1 pound fresh mixed mushrooms

6-inch piece kombu seaweed

2 ounces dried mixed mushrooms

3 leeks, white parts only, roughly chopped

6 green onions, roughly chopped

¼ cup sake

Water, as needed

2 tablespoons yellow miso paste

¼ cup tahini

1 tablespoon soy sauce

2 teaspoons chile paste

Preheat the oven to 350°F. Line a large rimmed baking sheet with aluminum foil.

In a bowl, toss the eggplants, onions, carrots, cabbage, garlic, and ginger with oil until coated on all surfaces. Pour the vegetables onto the prepared baking sheet. Roast the vegetables, turning occasionally, until they are well-charred on all sides, about 15 minutes. Remove the vegetables from the oven and drizzle with the fermented honey.

Transfer the vegetables to a large saucepan. Add the mushroom stems, kombu, dried mushrooms, leeks, and green onions. Add the sake and enough water to cover the vegetables, about 6 cups. Bring the liquid to a boil over medium-high heat, then reduce the heat so the liquid just simmers. Simmer until aromatic and flavorful, about 2 hours.

Strain the broth through a fine-mesh sieve into a clean large saucepan. Add the miso and tahini, soy sauce, and chile paste and stir to blend. Pour the stock into clean, quart-sized canning jars with lids. Cool the broth before sealing with the lids and store in the refrigerator. The broth will remain good for 3 days under refrigeration.

HOMEMADE SOYMILK

MAKES ABOUT 3½ CUPS

We only use organic soy products to avoid any of the pesticide controversy associated with commercial soy foods. It's easier for us to keep soybeans in the pantry and make this milk fresh between long periods of trips to town.

1 cup organic soybeans

3 quarts water

Medium piece of cheesecloth

Soak the soybeans overnight at room temperature in 2 quarts of the water. In the morning, drain the soybeans and rinse with cold water.

In a saucepan, heat 1 cup of the water over medium heat. While the water is heating, combine the remaining 3 cups water and the soaked, rinsed soybeans in a blender and process until the mixture is very smooth, about 3 minutes. Add the soybean puree to the warming water and turn the heat to medium-high. Warm the mixture until a foam starts to rise, about 5 minutes. Stir often to make sure the mixture doesn't stick to the pan.

Pour the mixture into a strainer lined with moistened cheesecloth suspended over a bowl. Twist the top of the cheesecloth until it begins to tighten and push against the strainer and squeeze until all the liquid has drained into the bowl.

Return the liquid to the (rinsed out) pot and bring it to a boil over medium heat for 8 minutes, stirring the bottom of the pot to prevent burning.

Remove the milk from the heat and transfer to any desired container to cool. Cover and refrigerate until ready to use.

SPRUCE SUGAR

MAKES 2 CUPS

The smell of this sugar brings the forest into the kitchen. We use spruce sugar on cookies, on cakes, and on savory dishes. We also use it sometimes in fancy cocktails at the bar. You can find spruce tips through online sources.

1 cup fresh spruce tips, brown paper caps removed

1 cup sugar

Preheat the oven to 225°F. Line a rimmed baking sheet with parchment paper.

Place the spruce tips and sugar into a food processor. Pulse a few times until the spruce tips are broken down somewhat, but not so much that the sugar becomes powdered.

Spread the spruce-sugar mixture over the prepared baking sheet. Place in the oven and bake until the mixture is completely dry; this will take between 1 hour and several hours, depending on the humidity in your area and the sugar. Remove from the oven and let cool.

As soon as it has cooled, transfer the spruce sugar to a clean glass jar with a tightly fitting lid. It will keep for up to 6 months.

SWEET SESAME CRUNCH

MAKES ABOUT 1 CUP (10 OUNCES)

We sprinkle this crumbly mixture on desserts, appetizers, and even savory dishes. Sesame goes with practically everything, and, as you can tell from our recipe collection, it's a staple in our kitchen.

1 cup sugar

¼ cup honey

½ teaspoon sea salt

3 tablespoons water

1 cup raw sesame seeds

1 teaspoon pure vanilla paste or vanilla extract

2 teaspoons unsalted butter

¼ teaspoon baking soda

Line a rimmed baking sheet with a silicone baking mat.

In a high-sided saucepan over medium heat, combine the sugar, honey, salt, and water. Whisk until just blended. Cook the mixture, stirring often, until the mixture turns a light caramel color, or until it reaches 280°F on a candy thermometer, 5 to 10 minutes. Add the sesame seeds and continue to cook until the mixture reaches 300°F. Immediately remove the pan from the heat and carefully stir in the vanilla and butter. Once the butter has completely melted, stir in the baking soda. Be careful: the mixture will foam up a bit and will be very hot.

Pour the mixture out onto the prepared baking sheet and let stand until completely cooled and hardened, about 20 minutes.

Break the cooled and hardened crunch into small pieces. Store the crunch in a sealed glass jar and use it within 1 month.

TART SHELL

MAKES ONE 10-INCH TART SHELL

This is a good, all-purpose pastry crust that we use for all of our sweet tarts. It's easy to put together, and the dough can be made ahead of time and refrigerated or frozen to roll out and fill on another day. It's important to keep the dough very cold in order to retain the desired flaky texture.

Canola oil for greasing
1 cup all-purpose flour, plus extra for dusting
1 tablespoon sugar
½ teaspoon sea salt
½ cup chilled unsalted butter, cut into small pieces
1 large egg, beaten

Preheat the oven to 400°F. Grease a 10-inch fluted tart pan with a removable bottom.

Place the flour, sugar, and salt into a food processor. Pulse a couple of times to mix the ingredients. Add the butter pieces and pulse until a rough dough forms. Add the egg and pulse just until the dough comes together. Wrap the dough tightly (we like to use Bee's Wrap and then aluminum foil) and refrigerate for 15 minutes.
You can also freeze the dough at this point for up to 4 weeks. Thaw in the refrigerator before using.

Place the dough on a lightly floured work surface. Using a rolling pin, roll the chilled dough to a round ¼-inch thick. Carefully transfer the dough to the prepared tart pan and gently press the dough into the sides. Trim the edges and freeze the trim for future use. Refrigerate the dough in the pan for 15 minutes.

Remove the tart pan from the refrigerator and cover the dough with parchment paper. Add dried beans (or other pie weights) on top of the paper and press the paper and weights into the edges. Bake for 20 minutes, then carefully lift out the beans and paper.

Let the tart shell cool completely on a wire rack before filling.

XO SAUCE

MAKES 2 CUPS

XO sauce is a spicy, Chinese-style seafood-based sauce that adds lots of umami to dishes. We had a chef one year that would add in garden-picked cilantro leaves to his XO sauce. It was so delicious. You can find dried fish in Asian markets or dry your own in the oven. We have good Alaska-grown cured pork products these days, but we will never turn down Iberico or Serrano ham.

½ cup canola oil
2 tablespoons red pepper flakes
¼ pound cured ham, minced
2 shallots, minced
2 cloves garlic, minced
1-inch knob fresh ginger, peeled and minced
2 bird's eye chiles, seeded and finely diced
¼ cup dried shrimp, soaked in water overnight and drained
¼ cup dried scallops, soaked in water overnight and drained
2 tablespoons chopped nori seaweed
1 cup store-bought or homemade chicken stock
2 tablespoons tomato paste
½ teaspoon honey
¼ cup Thai fish sauce (nam pla)
2 tablespoons dark mushroom soy sauce
½ teaspoon freshly ground black pepper

In a sauté pan over medium-high heat, combine the oil and pepper flakes. When the flakes are actively sizzling, add the ham, shallots, garlic, ginger, and chiles. Sauté until the ham is crisp, about 1 minute. Add the drained seafood and nori and cook just until aromatic, about 30 seconds.

Transfer the contents of the pan to a food processor and pulse until a chunky paste forms. Return the mixture to the pan, scraping out the workbowl with a rubber spatula, and place over low heat. Add the chicken stock and tomato paste and cook down for 1 minute. Stir in the honey, fish sauce, mushroom soy sauce, and black pepper.

Transfer the sauce to a clean glass canning jar with a lid. Store the XO sauce in the refrigerator for up to 1 month.

INDEX

Note: Page references in *italics* indicate photographs.

ACKNOWLEDGMENTS

We'd like to thank all of our guests who share in our culinary adventures. They allow us to do the work we love.

Tim Crockett, our R&D chef, spent much time with us testing recipes on this project. We are thankful for his hard work and creative expertise.

We appreciate all the remarkable and talented photographers who have spent time with us—in boats, and planes, helicopters, dog sleds; on the ocean and on mountaintops. Your photos allow us to tell our story and we are forever grateful for your friendship.

We sincerely appreciate Jennifer Newens and Rachel Metzger from the West Margin Press team for their grace, patience, and guidance through the collaborative process.

We also appreciate the hard-working Alaskan farmers and fishers we surround ourselves with, giving us beautiful food for our tables.